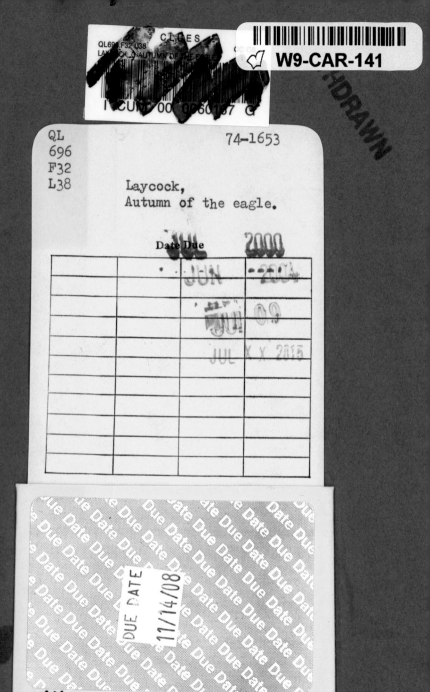

AUTUMN OF THE EAGLE

AUTUMN OF THE EAGLE

George Laycock

ILLUSTRATED WITH PHOTOGRAPHS AND MAPS

New York

CHARLES SCRIBNER'S SONS

Contents

A Portfolio of Pictures   7

Foreword   31

1. The National Bird   37

2. The Vanishing Wilderness   52

3. The Eagle Family   59

4. The Eyrie   75

5. The Eagles of Vermilion   88

6. A Matter of Diet   97

7. The Champion Eagle Bander   107

8. Danger in the Sky   122

9. The Chemical Age   132

10. A Search for Eagles   147

11. Intolerance and Poison   160

12. Shotguns and Helicopters   *178*

13. Land of Many Eagles   *192*

14. First Aid and Deep Concern   *201*

15. What of the Future?   *212*

     Reference Notes   *223*

     Selected Bibliography   *232*

     Acknowledgments   *234*

     Index   *235*

A Portfolio of Pictures

The majestic bald eagle, recognizable when mature by its gleaming white head and tail, has been the symbol of the United States since 1782

OPPOSITE. A cousin of the American bald eagle, the African fish eagle, boldly marked in brown, white, and black, lives along rivers, lakes, and seacoasts and feeds almost exclusively on fish

Pioneering scientist and photographer, Dr. Francis H. Herrick, along the south shore of Lake Erie, was the first to study the life history of the bald eagle in detail

OPPOSITE. This tower brought Dr. Herrick and his co-workers to eye level with the nesting eagles. A tent on the platform hid the observers from the eagles' view

From his high-rise observation point Dr. Herrick watched adult eagles deliver fish from Lake Erie to the hungry young in the nest

OPPOSITE. This giant nest, more than 12 feet deep and weighing an estimated 2 tons, was made famous by Dr. Herrick's studies

As an eagle's nest becomes older and heavier, the tree supporting it may die and fall, as did this ancient elm on the shore of Lake Erie

OPPOSITE. An adult bald eagle breaks its speed and descends for a landing on an unusual clifftop nest

On the treeless Aleutian Islands, eagles build their nests on the edge of grass-covered cliffs; this one is on Amchitka Island

As they grow and their feathers develop, young eagles spend much time preening

OPPOSITE. Fully feathered and as large as its parents, this young eagle exercises on its nest in preparation for the day when it will lift itself into the sky for its first flight

OPPOSITE. As the young eagle gains strength and confidence, the nest provides a platform on which to leap about and sometimes launch into short experimental flights

Retired banker Charles Broley marked more than 1200 young eagles with official aluminum leg bands, sometimes banding 150 in a single season

Broley used a rope ladder of his own design to climb to eagle nests, some as high as 125 feet above the ground

OPPOSITE. Once in the nest, Broley completed his banding quickly, then departed, leaving the eyrie to its owners

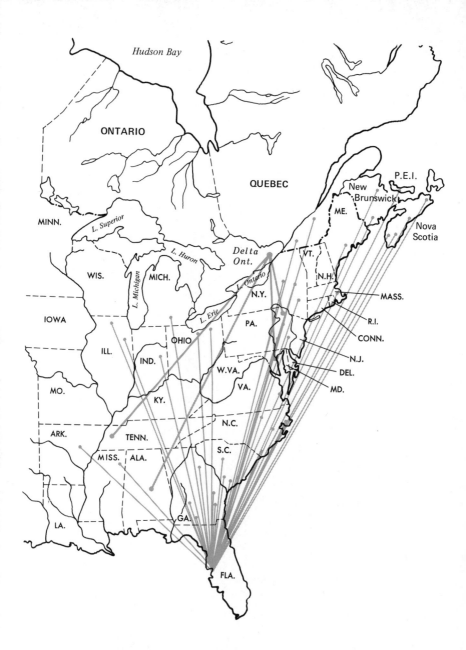

Bands applied by Broley in Florida were sent back from the northern and western locations shown, solving the mystery of where the eagles went for the summer

In the Chippewa National Forest in northern Minnesota, an eagle bander climbs a giant pine to band two young eagles

Nestling eagles are large enough to band before they are fully feathered. The bands used are of a special interlocking design difficult for the birds to remove

OPPOSITE. Bald eagles are still numerous in parts of Alaska, including Amchitka Island where this photograph was taken

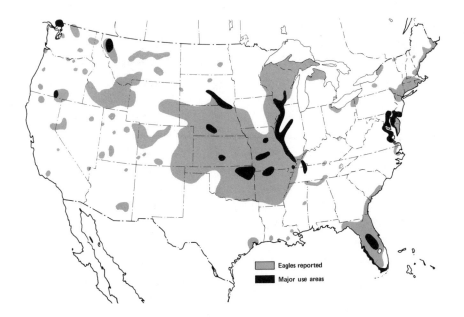

Bald eagle distribution, January. The map was made by biologists on the basis of nationwide surveys to learn where bald eagles concentrate in winter

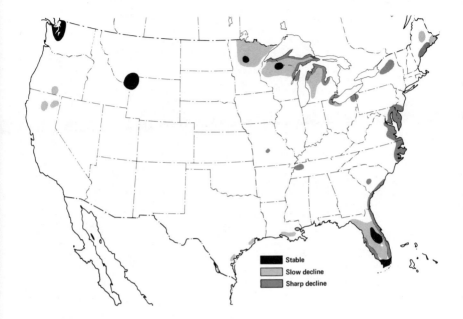

A search of the continental United States from land, water, and air in 1966 showed that active nests of the bald eagle were found only in the shaded areas on the map

Although eagles are fully protected by law, each year an unknown number fall victim to the guns of irresponsible men; this one was shot in Michigan

OPPOSITE. The golden eagle, the only other eagle living wild in North America, resembles the immature bald eagle but can be distinguished by the complete feathering of its lower legs

The bald eagle that once soared on strong wings above the American sea coasts, major rivers, and inland lakes, has vanished from much of its historic range and faces an uncertain future

Foreword

THERE comes a season when the last pair of eagles casting their gliding shadows on the lonely shores of Lake Erie patrol the shallow waters without ever catching a glimpse of any others of their kind. The eagles that once occupied territories to the east and to the west are no longer remembered. One autumn day the old pair sees a single young eagle winging southward, but it passes on and out of sight. Do eagles sense the growing emptiness of the eagle's skies? Are eagles at ease when there is no limit to their territory, no place where another of their kind will challenge them? Or are eagles a stimulus to other eagles, a force to help keep all eagles competitive, alert, and able?

The old pair had raised no young during the summer, nor even produced any eggs. It was the same as it had been the year before, and the year before that. Each spring, in a bright promising flurry of activity, they had searched the countryside for fresh sticks and carried them to the top of the old tree to repair and strengthen the nest which they had claimed for so many years. But with this done their lethargy returned, courtship was aborted, and their breeding cycle again failed to add a single new eagle to the dwindling population.

Then, during the early days of November, the male, old now but still strong in flight and bold in appearance, flew low over a barnyard several miles to the east, and from near the barn a figure appeared. A gun was lifted, and before the eagle understood, or even heard the noise, he tumbled helplessly toward the earth, where he died. No male eagle remained along all the southwest shore of Lake Erie.

His mate stayed in the neighborhood for two weeks, sitting for long silent hours, scarcely moving in the top of her favorite tree, where the old male had once rested near her. Sometimes she made short purposeless flights but returned to sit statuelike for hours on the perch while the cold winds of early winter buffeted her. Once every day or two she patrolled the beach until she discovered a white-bellied fish lying dead on the yellow sand, picked it up, returned to her perch, and fed. Then, at last, some strange force stirred within her, and she lifted heavily from her perch in the middle of an autumn morning when the sun and the wind had dried the world, and the breezes of the broad lake gave support to her powerful wings. She flew now toward the west and the south, following rivers as she came to them. At night she roosted in woodlots as far as possible from farmhouses, towns, or highways, and always as she traveled she stayed well above the earth where the elevation gave her a strong sense of safety.

She came at last to the big river and traveled down the stream until she arrived at the dam. There she perched silently above the edge of the river in the top of a giant dying elm tree and studied the gulls, mallards, scaup, and the few small teal down from the north.

Two days later the old eagle, while perched in the tree, caught her first glimpse of a young male coming along the river from the north. Her powerful eyes identified him long before the human eye might have told what manner of big bird he was, and she watched him intently as he drew closer. He was flying high and appeared to be passing on down river paying the old female scarcely any attention. She called once to him in her shrill piercing voice, but received no answer. Finally, she pushed from her perch and began climbing the skies on the trail of the younger bird, and keeping him always in view, she gained steadily on him.

At the next dam the young bird gave up altitude and settled gradually toward the treetops. By now the old female was flying close beside him. She came to a perch a hundred feet upstream from where the young male had alighted. He was not yet wearing adult plumage. Both his head and tail were splotched with brown and white, and perhaps would be for another full year. But he was a large bird, and he flew with the strength of youth and with the sureness of one who had traveled this river route before.

For two days the eagles stayed around the dam, feeding together. Then the newly formed pair, the female slowed by age and the male possessed of the strength and vigor of the young, moved northward up the river valleys, drawn by the strong bonds of the female back toward her empty waiting nest. But the years were a weight upon her.

No longer would she rise far into the sky. Nor would she half-fold those long broad wings and plunge out of the sky to snatch an injured mallard from the water. Her motions grew slower and more deliberate until one morning, still a hundred miles short of the old nest beside the great lake, she did not take to the sky.

All day she sat hunched on a perch near the top of an ancient sycamore beside the river while the young male made short flights as if to coax her into the air. Each time he would return and perch near her and wait. During the night she tumbled from the tree and fell dead beneath the sycamore.

Her youthful mate stayed in the vicinity most of that day. No other eagles came into view. He was free of the bonds of territory and bound to no other of his kind. As he climbed the gray, cold sky of early winter, he circled once, called in his shrill, piercing voice, and changed his course, flying back toward the big river from which she had led him.

AUTUMN OF THE EAGLE

1

The National Bird

WE met early on a brisk, beautifully clear morning in June, a climber, a biologist, and a writer searching for an eagle tree. For an hour our boat wound through narrow channels of clear water, across small open lakes, and along the dark forests that grow down to the water's edge. Lacy patterns of sloughs and creeks were woven into watery networks, the headwaters of the Mississippi flowing southward to form a river deserving of the name. On these cold, lonely waters our boat surprised families of mallards, red-necked grebes, and occasionally a loon that plunged beneath the surface to bob up a hundred feet behind us. We skirted shallow waters where wild rice lay on the surface in a pattern of pale green lines pointing with the current.

We slid through a narrow neck of water and rounded a point; the motor grew quiet as the boat drifted. "Up there in that big pine," the biologist said, handing me his binoculars, "you can see them perched on that limb to the left of the nest."

I adjusted the binoculars and found the nest and the pair of adult birds, still half a mile away. While I watched, one of the birds heaved itself from the perch and flew off slowly across the water. As we moved closer to the nest tree, the other bird lifted itself on broad dark wings, and both of them began a nervous circling flight back and forth across their territory, which we had invaded.

Those powerful wings, more than 6 feet from tip to tip, lifted up and down with a strong rhythmic beat that carried the 10- to 12-pound eagles through the air with grace and confidence. The eagle is master of the air, and flying against the deep blue backdrop of the Minnesota sky the pair of adults etched an unforgettable image. To watch an eagle is to be transported as if by magic quickly and surely back into a time when waters still ran clean, skies were clear, and forest, fields, and streams were sanctuaries to abundant wild creatures.

Today we see only rare reminders of that wilderness, a line of trumpeter swans skimming over the broad wetlands of the Centennial Valley in southwestern Montana; the massive bull elk bugling in the golden autumn sunshine of an alpine meadow; the yellowish bulk of the barrenland grizzly on the tundra in Alaska's Brooks Range. There are others: a giant alligator in Louisiana; or a family of whooping cranes in Texas—all creatures of the wild. But none is more memorable than the magnificent eagle.

The nest we had discovered was in a red pine tree on an island in the lake, a full 90 feet above the ground. The climber knew the tree from previous years—it was not a difficult one to climb, but not especially easy, either. Overhead the fretting eagles flew back and forth, calling continuously in strident protest. They flew in broad sweeps across the island, sometimes continuing for a quarter of a mile or more before turning back, their brilliant white tails and heads flashing in the early morning sunlight. A few times one of them alighted on a prominent perch in the top of a tree, only to launch itself quickly into the air again and rejoin its mate. They kept their distance, and I was reminded of the words of Edward H. Forbush: "An adult eagle usually has enough sad experiences with mankind to teach it circumspection."[1]

As we watched the eagles, the wildlife biologist John Mathisen told us the story of bald eagles in the Chippewa National Forest, where he works and where we were now traveling. This forest, spread across 1.65 million acres of northern Minnesota, is blanketed by conifers, aspen, and northern hardwoods. More than twelve hundred lakes lie within its boundaries, and these waters harbor walleyes, northern pike, muskellunge, perch, and white fish, predators in their own right, but food in turn for the eagles.

Within this flat, forested land lives one of the few remaining sizable populations of wild bald eagles still to be found anywhere in the United States outside of Alaska. Because it is an important last stronghold of the national bird, the Chippewa is an outdoor laboratory where biologists study the eagle's life.[2]

John began his detailed probing into the life of the Chippewa eagles by ground level searches in 1963. In summer, others arrived to help in the eagle study. Dr. Alfred Grewe, Jr., brought student aides from St. Cloud College, St. Cloud, Minnesota. Joel Kussman, Greg Juenemann, and Dr. Thomas Dunstan all joined in the nesting study, along with Dr. L. D. Frenzel, Jr., of the University of Minnesota, and some of Dr. Frenzel's students. John Mathisen, as he traveled around the area, talked with local residents who often provided clues to eagles' whereabouts. The first year he located forty-eight active nests. In succeeding years, the number of known nests increased gradually, not because more eagles were building nests, but because John and those searching with him were more successful in finding them. By 1965 he was flying over the area at low altitudes, searching out the nests and attempting to count the young. In June, when the young are large enough to band, he and his climber, Jack Stewart, decorate as many eaglets as possible with official, numbered, aluminum legbands issued by the United States Bureau of Sport Fisheries and Wildlife. From this they can learn of mortality rates, migration patterns, and life expectancy.

Just getting to an eagle's nest tree can be a major production. Often the men must travel by foot and canoe for several miles through shallow water, forests, bogs, and tag alder thickets where mosquitoes swarm around them ceaselessly. On the day that I was with them, John and I watched as Jack fought his way through the thick-growing underbrush toward the base of the towering red pine tree.

Jack is a slender, quiet-speaking, bone-hard woodsman who has seen the landscape from the tops of countless trees. He takes them as they come, pines, aspen, maples, whatever grows in the North Woods and needs climbing. He fitted his climbing irons to his legs, tightened the straps that bound them in place, and attached two heavily buckled belts to his waist. Slung over his back was an ancient gray-green packsack in which he carried aloft his camera and a few essential tools including a ring of strong aluminum legbands and pliers for attaching them. In addition, he carried a thin, stout line. If an eaglet, startled by its first glimpse of a man's face peering over the lip of the nest, should leap for the first time from its sky platform and flutter to the ground, the climber was prepared to lower the canvas bag to his nonclimbing friend, then hoist the young bird once more to the security of its eyrie.

Jack had volunteered for the job. He liked climbing, and in the absence of craggy mountain peaks the eagle tree became his challenge. He climbed with sureness and a sense of purpose. His skill was acquired during years of working for the United States Forest Service, climbing to the tops of spruces and pollinating the trees in selective breeding experiments.

He gets a spectacular view from that perch in the sky. Resting against the edge of the huge nest, or actually sitting in it with the young eagles, he can gaze far out across the endless woodlands and sparkling lakes, see the green forest and dark waters as the eagles know them, and rock in the gentle wind with the swaying of the pines. Jack explained that when he started this project he had known more about climbing than he did about eagles. He was, he insisted, not likely to forget his first climb to the eyrie of the eagle. John had reassured him: "Bald eagles do not attack men who climb to their nests." Jack reminded himself of this continuously as he cautiously ascended the tree while the pair of giant birds circled overhead, screeching in protest. "I peered over the edge of that huge nest," he recalled, "and wondered why I had ever volunteered for this job. I dug my climbing spurs into the big red pine, secured my safety belt, and slowly reached for one of those hissing eaglets. What I expected was to have one of them sink those sharp talons into my hand. John was right about the adults; they did not attack me. After banding the two youngsters, and taking a few pictures of them, I started that long climb back to the ground." Since then Jack has lost count of the number of eagle trees he has ascended.[3]

On the day of our expedition, John wanted to examine the young eagle in the first nest and check the stage of development of its feathers, so Jack put the youngster into his canvas sack and the fuzzy dark gray chick rode its elevator to earth. Except for a noisy clacking of its bill, it was a quiet and docile ball of down and big feet as John cradled it in his arm and banded it. Inspected, banded, and photographed, it was sent aloft again in excellent condition. Jack inched down the rough bark of the red pine a step at a time. "That was an easy one. I could work my way right up beside the nest on the limbs. Some of them you have to pull yourself up over and get right inside the nest. But these nests are big and strong. They'll almost always hold you."

Ahead of us was one more nest to be checked during the morning. We settled back into the boat and skimmed for half an hour over smooth water along the timbered shores. The second nest, like the first, was at least 90 feet above the ground, but since it was in a tree that stood on a small rise, the birds had spectacular elevation above the lake.

These eagles, like the first pair, flapped and glided far above us, calling down in constant protest. They made a magnificent and stirring picture as their clean white heads and tails flashed against the cobalt sky. Even John Mathisen and Jack Stewart, for whom bald eagles are a familiar sight, never grow weary of watching them.

At one time the bald eagle's range extended from the Florida Keys to the coast of Maine, and from Baja California to the Aleutian Islands. Some made their way across the turbulent Bering Sea to Bering Island, the only place beyond the North American continent where the wild bald eagle is found. Tens of thousands of them once built their nests and raised young eagles along the coasts of North America, beside the fish-producing rivers, and around the inland lakes. These magnificent giant birds, once kings of the skies, are now so rare that most Americans have never seen one, and in the future fewer yet will see them outside of zoos. "Our surveys," John said, "tell us that we have about 105 active nests in the Chippewa Forest. For all of the United States, outside Alaska, there are now only about 750 active nests."

This decline of the national bird began a long time ago, perhaps on the day the earliest settlers from Europe arrived on the American continent. Through the years the attrition has accelerated. Since World War II the eagle population has been declining at a frightening pace, until the extinction of the giant bird is threatened. This postwar development, as Alexander Sprunt IV, Director of Research for the National Audubon Society, has said, was "a very different sort of trend . . . a pronounced and accelerated loss of eagles." The eagles gradually disappeared from one locality after another, and the southern race was declared rare and endangered. Only in a few favored places can the national bird still be found living through its annual cycles with some success.[4]

John Mathisen's studies have shown that the bald eagle of the Chippewa produce 1.4 young per active nest, and there is some belief that even this rate of fledgling production is too low to maintain populations at their current levels.

Suddenly the future of the national bird is in jeopardy everywhere, except perhaps in parts of Alaska, and in one corner of Florida where resident eagles may still not have stored lethal levels of environmental poisons in their tissues.

Man's reverence for these regal birds of prey dates back to earliest human history. Primitive man, staring into the skies, marveled at the giant birds whose mysterious powers let them soar to the limits of human vision and beyond. They sailed the skies with a sense of freedom that, in the minds of the ancients, bridged the chasm between the world of man and the land of spirits. For this reason, eagles were released during the funeral rites of ancient Egyptians to bear the souls of deceased rulers to the heavens. The legions of Rome, marching behind the eagle's image, were neither the first nor the last to draw upon the form and majesty of these great symbolic birds for their inspiration.

Respect for the sacred character of the eagle permeated the religious and social beliefs of the North American Indians so deeply that, even today, eagle feathers are prized by dancers preserving the ancient ceremonial customs of their ancestors. The long feathers of the eagle wings worn on the arms added promise to the Pueblos' dance for rain and hope for peace to the dances of the

Iroquois. The feathers of the eagle spoke of rank and became badges of daring in battle and on the hunt. Some tribes, instead of killing the eagle, would keep it captive and remove only a few precious feathers at a time.

The Cheyenne brave killed the eagle for its feathers but did so only with strict attention to ancient ceremonial details, which included a formal apology to the spirit of the bird. The ritual was lengthy and demanding. The brave went into his lodge alone and through the long, dark night sang the sacred tribal chants reserved for the occasion. The following morning he emerged from his lodge to go into the plains and select the place for capturing the eagle, a place readily seen by the eagle in the sky. There he dug a hole in which to crouch and wait, but he dug with great care, working only when there were no eagles in sight, and carrying the earth away to avoid discovery of his plans by the sharp eyes of the eagle. Then he gathered long grass to lay over the pit as a roof.

On the day of the capture the warrior would bathe, then cover his body with oils to mask the man odor. Before the first yellow light of dawn he slipped off silently to crouch hidden in the pit beneath the brown grass. Above him, he placed a dead rabbit or other fresh bait, lashed down securely to prevent the eagle from swooping in and carrying it away.

At last the eagle would circle the blue morning sky, then come steadily and swiftly closer on its widespread wings. It would settle on the meat, begin tearing at it, and become so driven by its hunger that it would not see the brown hands reaching slowly up through the grass below it. Then the eagle would be dragged struggling and flap-

ping down into the pit. There, according to Cheyenne custom, it could be killed in only one manner, by strangulation
with a noose. Having taken eagles with his bare hands, the
brave could walk with great pride among his people. He
also gained a practical advantage, as the barter value of the
feathers was high. Twenty eagle feathers might pay for a
horse.[5]

The ancient respect for the eagles is reflected in the
symbolism of the American eagle. The image of the eagle
is imprinted on United States currency, is seen on pillars at
the entrances to public buildings, and is used to decorate
the walls of homes, offices, and public gathering places.
The eagle lends its name freely to fraternal orders, chemical industries, building and loan companies, towns, rivers,
ranches, and mountains. The eagle is commemorated in
the symbols of commerce and patriotism. One might think
that the choice of this king of wild birds as the national
symbol was inevitable, that no other creature could possibly compete with the eagle, so commanding in form, so
steeped in history. But as candidate for the national bird,
the eagle had its competitors and even its detractors.

At about two o'clock in the afternoon of July 4, 1776,
the members of the Continental Congress signed the Declaration of Independence. They then discussed what they
should do about an official seal, which would be the national coat of arms and would state to the world that this
nation had formally declared itself an independent sover-
eign republic. The Congress assigned three of its most
respected members to the task, men who had also played
major roles in writing the Declaration: "Resolved, That Dr.

Franklin, Mr. J. Adams and Mr. Jefferson be a committee to prepare a device for the Seal of the United States of America."[6]

As a beginning they might have drawn upon the seals already in use by various of the thirteen colonies. But instead of the relatively simple designs used in these seals, each member had his own somewhat grandiose concept. Dr. Franklin, according to a letter of John Adams to his wife, suggested a seal showing "Moses lifting up his hand and dividing the Red Sea, and Pharaoh in his chariot overwhelmed with the waters." Thomas Jefferson envisioned the seal as depicting the children of Israel in the wilderness, led by a cloud by day and a fire by night. As for himself, John Adams proposed an assemblage of characters from Greek mythology, then admitted that it was too complicated and "not original."[7]

With the help of a Philadelphia artist, the committee, after six weeks of agonizing debate, completed its report and submitted it to Congress. Congress, however, was unable to reach agreement, and the ill-fated report was tabled for four years, leaving the infant nation to manage as best it could without benefit of an official seal. In March 1780 the need was brought to the attention of Congress again and a second committee was handed the assignment. The report of this committee was tabled for two more years; then the perplexing task was given to a third committee. At this point the only lasting result of six years of discussion was the motto *E pluribus unum,* credited to Thomas Jefferson.

The third committee arranged for the services of artist William Barton, whose first sketch included an eagle. Barton, an expert on heraldry, knew that the eagle had been widely used through the centuries as a sign of invincibility —but his heraldic eagle bore little resemblance to any native American bird. Congress, still not satisfied with the design, and perhaps sensing by now that committee action was not an expeditious way to choose a national seal, simply handed the project over to its secretary, Charles Thomson. It was Thomson who elevated the eagle to its role as national bird. He made the eagle the central figure in his design, and insisted that it was to be an American bald eagle. In one talon the fierce looking bird carried an unlikely olive branch, in the other a bundle of arrows. Thomson and Barton refined the drawing, and within a week it was adopted by Congress as the Great Seal of the United States.

It was not, however, universally approved. One leader unconvinced of its merit was Benjamin Franklin, who, in a letter to his daughter in 1784, made plain his feelings about the American eagle. "For my part," he said, "I wish that the bald eagle had not been chosen as the representative of our country; he is a bird of bad moral character; he does not get his living honestly; you may see him perched on some dead tree, where, too lazy to fish for himself, he watches the labor of the fishing-hawk; when that diligent bird has at length taken a fish, and is bearing it to his nest for the support of his mate and young ones, the bald eagle pursues him and takes it from him." In addition, Dr. Franklin declared the eagle to be a coward and "often very lousy."

At this point Franklin made deprecating reference to the image of an eagle carried on the badges of the newly created Order of Cincinnatus. The figure, he insisted, looked more like a turkey than a bald eagle. This seemed to please him. "For in truth, the turkey," he said, "is in comparison a much more respectable bird, and withal a true native of America." The turkey, Franklin insisted, "might be more likely than the bald eagle to attack a grenadier of the British Guards should the soldier invade his farmyard with a red coat on."[8]

Inevitably, individual bald eagles have been remembered for their exploits. None, however, has gained more lasting fame, nor been more indelibly emblazoned on the pages of American history than a fabled eagle from northern Wisconsin that went south during the Civil War. This eagle would not have gone to war at all had it not been for a Chippewa Indian who one day in 1861 looked skyward and noted the broad form of an eagle nest in the top of a towering pine tree. The Indian, whose name was Sky Chief, decided he would like to have an eagle, and ignoring the angry protests of the circling adult birds, he began chopping on the base of the big pine tree. As the tree came crashing to earth, the young lone occupant of the nest was tossed free to flutter weakly in the underbrush, where it was eagerly pounced upon by the elated Sky Chief.

The eaglet proved to be less than an ideal pet. It showed constant signs of a nasty disposition, most often expressed in an effort to clamp its two sets of needle-sharp talons into the arms or face of its captor. Understandably, Sky Chief changed his mind about wanting an eagle. He was practical enough, however, to resist the urge to wring the evil-tempered bird's neck: as an item of barter the bird might bring some reward for all that chopping. When his father, Chief Thunder of Bees, made his next trip down the cold, clean waters of the Flambeau to sell craftwork items in the villages, Sky Chief and the eagle went along.

In the village of Eagle River, Sky Chief, proudly carrying his eagle, struck a trade with Daniel McCann, whose best offer was a bushel of yellow corn. "And for this paltry sum," an admirer wrote in later years, "was the noble bird sold from freedom to captivity . . . from the moans of the pines to the crash of battle, from obscurity to fame." McCann himself did not yet know precisely what he would do with an unfriendly bird possessed of a 7-foot wingspread and a pair of feet capable of disfiguring a man. But he had invested a bushel of corn in the deal, so he carried the eagle off to Chippewa Falls. There he sold it to the owner of a local store for $2.50, plus repeated assurance that the merchant would find his "pet" a good home.

Meanwhile, farm lads were trooping in from round about to join up with the Eau Claire Badgers, and the patriotic merchant presented the unit with a genuine American eagle. In honor of the president the soldiers named the young eagle "Old Abe," and henceforth "Old Abe," displaying a glaring countenance, rode atop a small square platform mounted on a pole and carried by James McGinnis, official keeper of this tethered king of the skies. The eagle on his platform rode at the head of his company with the color guard. Some reporters insisted that when people along the route of march applauded, the majestic eagle would spread his wings. Others made the questionable claim that on these occasions he picked up in his bill a small flag close by on his platform.

By the time Old Abe had been with the "Eagle Regiment" for several months, and his conditioning to military life was as complete as could be expected, he became, in addition to a noble symbol of his country's might, something of a damned nuisance. When free around the encampment he would amuse himself by slashing blue uniforms hung on the line to dry, upsetting soup pots, and generally causing trouble. He was, the soldiers said, "as spiteful as a scorpion" to all but McGinnis. But by the time he had served out his hitch he had become a hero credited with more acts of boldness, intelligence, and bravery than strict attention to detail could support.

During the summer of 1864 Old Abe, veteran of Vicksburg, Corinth, and other noted encounters, came home to Wisconsin with full honors, the most famous of all bald eagles. The handsome bird was formally presented to the governor of Wisconsin and allowed quarters in the basement of the state capitol.

Fame did not desert the aging eagle. In the years that followed, Old Abe was taken often from his room in the capitol building to make public appearances. He rose to the zenith of show business in 1876 when, with funds especially appropriated by the state legislature, he was sent to represent Wisconsin at the Philadelphia Exposition.[9]

Old Abe was twenty years old when he died of suffocation during a brief but smoky fire in the basement of the capitol. He has not to this day been forgotten. After death the honor accorded him was unique among the military figures to have served Wisconsin. He was mounted and displayed prominently in the state capitol, a constant reminder of the past when times were better for eagles.

2

The Vanishing Wilderness

On that historic day when the founding fathers chose the bald eagle as the symbol of their new government, the birds were, for the most part, blissfully unaware of approaching changes in their world. Along the south shore of Lake Erie, wilderness still surrounded the eagles, providing them privacy and giant columns of trees on which to secure their lofty platforms. No one can know how many pairs of eagles occupied eyries along Lake Erie in those years, but every few miles there was a giant nest in a towering tree, from which the eagles could look out across the lake.

These waters, clean, sweet, and fertile, harbored unimaginable tonnages of blue pike, walleyed pike, sturgeon, white bass, black bass, catfish, and perch. Seasonal hatches of mayflies changing from nymph to adult rose in milling, fluttering clouds from the lake, providing a brief banquet for birds and fish alike.[1]

On shore, the eagle trees belonged to a crowded community of towering broadleafed giants. Where the land was slightly higher maples and beeches grew, but much of the forest was a mixture of magnificent, straight tulip trees, mammoth black, red, and white oaks, and chestnuts, hickories, and others that had stood for hundreds of years. These forests defied simple classification by botanists because they were more than beech-maple, oak-hickory, or spruce-hemlock forest communities. The late Dr. Lucy Braun, of the University of Cincinnati, classified such forests as "mixed" mesophytic, meaning that they contain a wide variety of native species.[2]

Beneath the trees was spread a richness from which the giant plants drew strength and sustenance. The detritus, an accumulation of the dead parts of plants and animals, littered the forest floor to be attacked by millipedes, beetles, earthworms, springtails, and many others. In this world of the microscopic were billions of bacteria, protozoa, algae, and fungi by which nature returned its dead to the earth and produced more nourishment for the living. This spongy, moist layer was the living cradle of the forest seedlings.

Upon this rich earth, bushes, vines, ferns, and wildflowers competed for light and moisture beneath the forest canopy. From above the trees to beneath the earth's surface there lived countless species of insects, annelids, gastropods, amphibians, reptiles, birds, and mammals, each dependent upon the world around it and in turn depended upon for its role in the innumerable life cycles. This forest world, forged and tested over the centuries, had not yet been touched by the tools of man.

To the west lay vast marshlands, touching the lake on its westward shore, reaching inland in a 2-mile-wide band, and stretching out along the edge of the lake for 75 miles. These 300,000 acres were fed by the rivers that moved water north out of the Ohio country and emptied slowly into the shallow end of the lake, helping to form one of the richest ecosystems in the Great Lakes region. In autumn flourishing stands of wild rice, wild celery, pondweed, and smartweed attracted hundreds of thousands of mallards, black ducks, teal, scaup, canvasbacks, redheads, and other waterfowl. The waters supplied resident eagles with abundant food to support them and nourish their growing eaglets. From their perches or from the sky, the eagles surveyed the community of wild creatures that shared their wilderness. Within the forest below them lived stately elk, graceful white-tailed deer, ponderous bison, and the stealthy cougar. Black bears scratched their marks on the bark of the eagle tree. Flocks of skittish wild turkeys scratched the forest floor for acorns and roosted in the trees. Passenger pigeons streamed by in mile-wide flocks on wings that carried the sounds of the storm wind.[3]

The eagles and other wild creatures, living together in such profusion within the forests and along the streams and lakeshores, had seen no precipitous change in their world for thousands of years. The Indians changed it but little, while the French, who came to gather the wealth of furs of beaver and muskrat, scarcely changed it either. But others were soon to follow, to begin abruptly reshaping this wilderness world to their own needs.[4]

Thirty-eight miles west of the Cuyahoga River another river also flowed northward out of the forest to the lake. Near the mouth of this river were deposits of brilliant red clay, and Indian people made their way along the forest paths to gather the vermilion coloring for their paint. Eventually this clay would give its name to the Vermilion River, later to a town, and then to a famous eagle nest.

From their nest tree the Vermilion eagles, while still surrounded by wilderness, could see the river and the endless lake as today's eagles have never known it. Hunched low in the nest against the force of the chill lake winds, they heard at night only the sounds of the wilderness. Below them the calls of toads and frogs filled the night. The loon yodeled to its mate, the hunting fox barked, and the traveling wolf lifted its voice in doleful song. Behind it all were the sounds of the wind and of the waves breaking on the lakeshore. Black was the basic color of the night, softened only by the light of the moon, the sparkle of the stars, or the occasional flash of lightning.

Along that south shore of Lake Erie the world of the wild creatures was beginning to change character early in the 1800s. Along the Ohio River, civilization was already becoming well established, but for 120 miles westward from the border of Pennsylvania the wilderness was a fortress. These were the Western Reserve lands claimed by the Connecticut Land Company. In 1796 that company had dispatched a party of surveyors to its Lake Erie holdings with instructions to the leader, General Moses Cleaveland, to locate and lay out the site for a town. They came through the forest of widely spaced trees to the mouth of the Cuyahoga, a clean-running little river that began in north-

ern Ohio, flowed south, then doubled back in a horseshoe
100 miles long to empty its waters into Lake Erie.[5]

No sooner did General Cleaveland's crew of frontier
axmen and surveyors complete their task than they turned
homeward toward Connecticut, eager to leave the swampy,
insect-ridden lands along the big lake.

In the deep timberlands to the south an occasional
woodsman and his family eked out a living by parasitizing
the forest ecosystem. Sometimes they traveled all summer,
arrived too late in the year to build a cabin, and spent their
first winter in the strange and hostile land huddled together in a lean-to before a fire.

Then would come a small log home with earthen floor
and no windows. The ax and the gun were the tools of the
frontier: the skilled axman made furniture, felled trees,
trimmed logs, and made white oak splits for weaving bas-
kets. Bed might be a pile of leaves in the corner of the
cabin. Meat was harvested from the wild supplies. There
was no link with the outside world, no money for purchases
if there had been places to buy.

Next came the first of the farmers, choosing the higher
ground and laboring to clear it of its staggering growth of
tall timber. Like the Indian farmers before them, they gir-
dled the oaks, hickories, walnut, and tulip trees, then
waited for them to die. Eventually the "deadening" was
complete and the timber either fell in the storms or was
burned. Corn was planted in the thick loam that had nourished the towering trees.[6]

At the turn of the century, a single family, that of
Lorenzo Carter, was in residence in Cleaveland (its spelling
had not yet been changed) and the total population was

eight. This was the beginning of a time when men attacked the wilderness as they would an enemy, with a rapidity seldom rivaled in the peopling of a new land. Thirty-eight miles to the west, at the mouth of the Vermilion River, and within sight of the eagle's nest, the first settlement of Vermilion began in 1808.[7] Ten years later Lake Erie's first steamboat, a tiny craft called *Walk-on-the-water,* chugged into Cleveland at her top speed of 5 miles an hour, and heralded a new age of growth for the changing lakeshore.[8] But the greatest impact of all was the completion in 1827 of the Cleveland-to-Akron leg of the Erie Canal and the low-cost transportation it made possible. Increasingly, the forests fell crashing to earth, and the blue haze of the burning brush cast half-shadows over the lake country. Wilderness was the enemy of men wherever they came to live on the frontier. Everything that threatened, or appeared to threaten, the welfare of a man was frontally attacked with the weapons at hand. This applied not only to the forests but also to the wild creatures.

For the frontiersman the eagles, abundant and often in full view, served no useful purpose and would be removed from the scene along with other predators as opportunity presented. But even more than the killing of individual birds by gunfire, the change in the nature of the land would bring trouble to the eagle. Congress might declare the American bald eagle the national symbol, but the giant bird had been given no special protection by elevation to its symbolic status—nor, for that manner, did it appear to need such protection, at first. But to the pioneer, the wilderness was there to be conquered.

As the world changed from wilderness to farms and

villages, all interlinked with roads, railroads, and waterways, the eagle population diminished. At the mouth of the
Vermilion River the eagles stayed on and were known for
years to the people who lived in the sleepy village. The
eagles were in residence when the pleasure boats, one of
them named *The American Eagle,* made weekly stops at the
harbor in Vermilion during the 1800s.[9] They were there
into the 1900s, when the earliest automobiles began to
travel along routes that had once been Indian trails. But
eagles are vanishing now, along with the rest of the vanishing wilderness.

3

The Eagle Family

AROUND the world eagles display considerable variety in size, markings, and habits. They range in size from the little eagle of Australia and New Guinea to the splendid and powerful harpy eagle, a supreme avian predator that lives in the rain forests of Central and South America. The female may weigh up to 20 pounds and measure 3 feet from tail to bill. In the Philippines there is another giant forest-dwelling eagle that subsists primarily on flying lemurs and monkeys; it is almost as large as the South American harpy. But the monkey-eating eagles, victims of collectors and trophy hunters, number perhaps fewer than a hundred individuals. This bird is listed as an endangered species in the Red Data Book of the International Union for the Conservation of Nature.

The eagle is a diurnal bird of prey, classed with the hawklike birds, of which, worldwide, there are some 280 species including (in addition to hawks and eagles), vultures, kites, buzzards, falcons, and harriers. There are about 58 species of eagle (ornithologists disagree on the exact number). There are eight species of sea eagle—which characteristically make their homes around fairly large bodies of water and live largely on fish—all in the genus *Haliaeetus.* The American bald eagle is the only sea eagle native to North America.[1]

The largest of the sea eagles is a giant bird named for Georg Wilhelm Steller, a naturalist who in 1741 sailed from Russia with Vitus Bering to discover the Aleutian Islands. Steller's eagle is a striking, unforgettable northern giant weighing up to 19 pounds. It is equipped with a remarkably large, yellow bill; the adult's white shoulders, tail, and thighs contrast with its generally dark plumage. It is at home by the edges of the sea and beside larger rivers and lakes. It is found on dark craggy rocks along the coast of northeast Siberia and along rivers and inland lakes in forested regions. On rare occasions it is found as far east as the Pribilof Islands off the Alaska coast. Like its eastern cousin, the bald eagle, Steller's eagle sometimes congregates in winter along salmon streams to subsist upon spawning and dying fish. Like other sea eagles it commonly selects large trees to hold its bulky nest. There it raises its family year after year, an annual cycle beginning when the mated pair soars over the nest during the cold March days of earliest spring, calling to each other in loud unmusical notes.

Meanwhile, in Norway, Greenland, parts of Asia, and elsewhere the nesting of the white-tailed sea eagle is under way. The adults of this species have a flashy white tail contrasting with the deep brown of their plumage, and their coloring is somewhat lighter than that of their young. Through large sections of its range this eagle has been relentlessly persecuted for many decades, largely because of what shepherds insist is its propensity for killing sheep. In the British Isles, where it was once prominent, this persecuted sea eagle is now extinct.

The white-tailed sea eagles in Germany have been decimated by shooting and pesticides. Of the four pairs nesting in northwestern Germany in 1972, two failed to hatch any young, and a vandal climbed 60 feet to reach the eyrie of the third pair and kill the downy, helpless chick when it was two days old. The fourth pair produced a single eaglet, which lived to fly successfully from the nest—the only one that year to do so in all of western Europe outside Scandinavia.[2]

Another of the sea eagles, one that has been studied in less detail than most, is Sanford's sea eagle, a native of the Solomon Islands. This eagle, considerably smaller than the bald eagle, not only lives along the coasts, but has also adapted to life in the lowland forests of its islands. In these forests it has turned away from the sea eagles' normal diet of fish to subsist primarily on birds and mammals. The adult is a handsome, dark-colored bird with feathers that are a mixture of black and brown.

The African fish eagle is a striking bird easily seen around such places as Lake Naivasha, Lake Manyara, and Murchison Falls. Its flashing snow-white head and neck and its pure white tail are in sharp contrast to the black of its wings and the brown of its belly and shoulders. Its underparts are mostly white or slate gray. This eagle, one of the smallest sea eagles, is adept at catching live fish, but like other sea eagles, it does not restrict its diet to fish. It may sometimes be seen far inland around shallow pools.[3]

The Madagascar fish eagle is a dark brown bird with considerable white showing on its head and tail. It is somewhat smaller than the bald eagle, takes much of its food alive, and depends largely on fish.

The Pallas sea eagle, equal of the bald eagle in size, is often found around the inland waters of Central Asia, far from the sea. If it must, the Pallas eagle catches living fish, but like the bald eagle, it seems more inclined to feast, when possible, on food found already dead. Its nest, used year after year, is large and bulky, built either in large trees or on the ground. Its coloring is primarily brown, with the mature birds marked by a dark terminal band across the tail.

The white-bellied sea eagle, nearly as large as the bald eagle, is primarily a coastal species that lives in southern Asia and Australia. It is grayish brown and white, with white showing on the undersides and the head. The white-bellied eagle takes fish, and sometimes birds, but it has a special fondness for sea snakes. It surprises a snake as it rises to the surface for air, plucks it squirming from the water, and quickly kills it by clamping the snake's head in its powerful talons. The nest of the white-bellied sea eagle is a large collection of sticks, usually built in a tall tree. It lays two, or sometimes three eggs, to be incubated primarily by the female with an occasional assist by her mate.

The United States' national bird, the bald eagle, is one of the largest of the sea eagles. It is one of only two eagles that are residents of North America. The other, the golden eagle found around the world in the northern hemisphere, was a favorite of ancient royal falconers, as it is of modern admirers of the birds of prey. In the United States the golden eagle lives largely in the mountains and open prairies of the western states, where instead of hunting the waters for food it feeds primarily on land birds and mammals, especially rabbits. The golden eagle is more uniformly dark in color than the bald eagle; it does not have a white head and tail. It resembles the immature bald eagle, but they can be told apart by the leg feathers: those of the bald eagles come only to 2½ or 3 inches from the toes, while those of the golden eagle cover the entire leg.[4]

There is no difference between the coloring and marking of the male and female bald eagle. Their sexual dimorphism is limited to their difference in size, and as in the case with other birds of prey, the females are considerably larger than their mates. In size of wingspread, bald eagles are second only to the California condor among North American birds. The largest female bald eagles, 42 inches long and with a wingspread of more than 7 feet, may weigh from 10 to 16 pounds, while their smaller mates are perhaps 7 inches shorter, 2 or 3 pounds lighter, and equipped with wings only 6½ feet across. Their size varies geographically, with the largest of the species coming from the northern part of the range, the eagles of Alaska being noticeably larger than those of Florida. On this basis, scientists years ago separated the bald eagle into two subspecies, the southern bald eagle, *Haliaeetus leucocephalus leucocephalus*, and the northern bald eagle, *Haliaeetus leucocephalus alascanus*. The northern race is found largely in Canada and Alaska, the southern primarily south of the Canada–United States border. Search as they might, taxonomists can find no differences, except size, to justify this division of bald eagles into subspecies.

Eagles, like other birds, tend to die young, even under natural conditions. Today, with overpowering and pervasive environmental pollution, birds of prey face a greater possibility of dying young than ever before, while the numbers of nestlings are reduced from the beginning. The bald eagle that lives long enough to wear white on its head and tail can display them as a badge of success; it has survived the most hazardous period of its life. From then on, if it can elude the lawbreaking gunner and develop the unlikely ability to recognize and avoid chemically laden fish, it might survive to the age of 40 and leave descendants behind. Through those years, it is, like other eagles, a monogamist, taking a new mate only if its former mate dies.

As the newly hatched eaglet comes from the egg and dries, it is covered with down, smoky in color except for the head, which is white. For three weeks the chick wears this incredibly soft, thick, natal down, which is gradually replaced by a coat of darker and thicker woolly down. Before the young bird is able to rise and stand on two feet, it braces itself with its wingtips, moving about with an infant's wobbly and uncertain steps.

When the chick is 6 or 7 weeks old, the down is replaced by dark feathers, which appear first on wings and tail and finally cover the body. The eaglets grow on the abundant food carried to them, until their size equals or exceeds that of their parents, and as they grow toward full size the concern of the parents for their safety slowly diminishes. No longer do the young birds, covered with their new feathers and equipped with powerful talons, need constant protection from rain and sun, gulls and magpies, raccoons and red-tailed hawks. The nest-building urge of the parents also wanes. They gradually cease carrying sticks and grass to the tree for nest repairs as they did occasionally far into the summer.

The first feathers of the juvenile are dark brown, almost black, and they are worn through the remainder of the bird's first year. Bald eagles undergo one molt annually, beginning in spring and proceeding gradually through early autumn. In succeeding years white begins to appear on the head and tail, mixed at first with the dark brown, until in the fully adult state—in the eagle's fifth or sixth year—the dark chocolate brown contrasts sharply with the gleaming white of the head and tail. The voice of the eagle changes too, becoming deeper as the young bird matures.

Occasionally, an inquisitive scientist considering the mystery of a bird's feathers is driven by his curiosity to approach the subject after the manner of an accountant, as Pierce Brodkorb once did to record some remarkable statistics. Brodkorb was working one day in his laboratory at the University of Florida reducing the body of a yearling female bald eagle, found dead in the field, to a scientific study skeleton. Bordkorb meticulously counted its feathers, one at a time, left wing 1,234, right wing 1,369, tail 139, and the remainder, section by section, until he had counted them all, a total of 7,182. Then the feathers and down were weighed. The feathers totaled more than 16 percent of the bird's weight, and were more than twice as heavy as the eagle's strong and flexible skeleton.[5]

The scream—or screech—of the bald eagle is a rather loud, piercing call that has been likened to the squeak of a rusty hinge on a barn door. Those who study eagles at length sometimes learn to separate the male and female by the differences in their calls. The call of the alarmed male bald eagle has been variously transcribed as *kark-kark-kark*, *kweek-kik-ik-ik-ik,* and *kweek-a-kuk-kuk.*

As the bald eagle hunts, it displays remarkable natural gifts that equip it for survival. One is its pair of splendid long, broad wings, with the long primary feathers particularly well adapted to soaring flight. The trailing edges of the primary feathers are slotted near the tips, giving the bird good lift at slow soaring speeds. This feather shape also helps stabilize the bird, giving it a relatively smooth ride even in rough winds.

In addition, the deep yellow eyes of the eagle are among the finest in nature. The hunting bird, patrolling the lake from half a mile high, scans the dark water and the edge of the distant shore, alert for a motion, a form, or a color that might reveal its food. Suddenly it alters course, gains speed, and descends in a long direct line toward the sandy beach. At the final moment one yellow leg is lowered and the four flexible toes grip and lift the lifeless form of a 2-pound catfish from the shallows, where it has been washed during the night. In his *Birds of New York,* Howard E. Eaton tells of watching a bald eagle fly in a straight line directly to a fish 3 miles from where the eagle had first seen it.[6]

Such magnificent visual acuity is characteristic of the birds of prey, which possess the best vision in the world of vertebrates. The soaring eagle can see the form of a cottontail crouching so far away that the human eye would see nothing but grass, and can detect the movement of a fish close to the surface at incredible distances. The eyes of a 10-pound eagle may be equal in size to those of a 200-pound man. The hidden sockets of the eagle's globular eyes occupy much of the bird's head. The large eyes so crowd the sockets that there is little freedom of movement, and instead of moving its eyes to study objects the eagle, like other birds of prey, must turn its head.[7]

But size is not the whole story. The eyes of the eagle are vastly superior to human eyes both for distinguishing detail and for depth perception. The eye of the eagle contains not one fovea, or depression in the retina, as in the case of man, but two, each exceedingly more powerful and with better resolving power than that of the human. While one of these fovea is fixed to look to the side, the other within the same eye looks forward. These two forward-looking fovea bring the same object into sharp binocular vision. An eagle's vision is roughly that of a man looking through six-power binoculars. This is not so much because the eagle's eyes magnify, but because they give a clearer picture.

Having traveled widely in its search for food, and located it, perhaps at an amazing distance, the eagle must also possess equipment for capturing and killing its prey. The heavy, hooked bill, which looks so threatening, is more a tool than a weapon; it aids in tearing food into bite size. Falconers who handle eagles seldom worry greatly about injury from the eagle's bill, but they never underestimate the power of the tremendous talons, which pierce the vital organs of the prey and seem to lock onto the victim until life is gone. The falconer handling an eagle wears a heavy leather glove reaching almost to his elbow. Otherwise the needle-pointed talons, an inch and a half long or more, could pierce the flesh in a grip that could not be broken by hand. The foot of the eagle has four toes, three pointing forward and one—which is longer, stronger, and equipped with a longer claw—pointing backward. Together these form a viselike clamp with piercing inward-curving talons capable of cutting into vital parts of mammals, birds, fish, or reptiles.

In the instant the eagle's talons touch its prey, powerful tendons flex and draw the toes tight, driving the needle-pointed talons inward toward each other, and there they remain locked like ice tongs, with each movement of the struggling animal only helping to pull the talons deeper into its body. Sea eagles, as well as the fish-eating osprey, have tiny, projecting spikes on the bottoms of their toes as an aid in gripping slippery fish.

Some eagles may stay the year around in the vicinity of their nest, while others migrate. Those that depart are not motivated by force of habit, length of day, or falling temperatures but by the demand for food. When ice and snow lock up their summer territories, shutting off their sources of fish or other foods, they have no choice; they must go. Winter's arrival sets their schedule, and the date of their travels may vary from year to year. The immature birds, however, are wanderers. They normally depart earlier than the adults and are the last to return in spring, idling along the way as befits those who do not yet have the responsibilities of an eyrie.

Migration patterns of eagles may change from year to year as new sources of food come to their attention. In recent times an increasing percentage of the country's bald

eagles have concentrated in winter around dams and wildlife refuges along the Mississippi valley, taking advantage
of supplies of fish and wounded waterfowl that were not
always available there in such abundance.[8]

The winter lives of such eagles take on an apparently
simple pattern. They sleep, eat, and perch in idleness near
the water. In northeastern Illinois, where eagles feed
heavily on gizzard shad captured around the openings in
the ice, biologist William E. Southern studied their habits
by equipping them with miniature radio transmitters, and
found that he could follow the beeping signals easily at a
distance of 3 miles, and could sometimes detect signals at
distances up to 28 miles. From these experiments Southern
found that eagles away from their nesting territories move
about in winter, and that even when food is plentiful in an
area they may depart (perhaps on a day when the thermals
are well suited to soaring), end up many miles away, and
not return. With no strong bonds holding them to any area,
winter becomes a time of wandering.

Radio tracking also helped Southern understand how
the birds roost and how they spend their daylight hours. As
night approaches they move to wooded roosting areas,
sometimes many miles from where they feed. They may
even pass up more convenient sources of food to travel
back and forth between familiar roosting and fishing areas.
They spend the night in tall trees, and at daylight they leave
the roost, flying sluggishly on the dead morning air, to
arrive one by one around the open waters. There, after
perhaps a quick pass over the water, an eagle may settle on
a perch and rest for half an hour before it begins to feed.
During the day the eagles continue to feed, some departing

and others arriving; by late afternoon, their numbers are thinning again as they fly off to roost.[9]

Unless they are hunting, bald eagles seem to take little notice of other wild species around them. Smaller birds such as crows, jays, kingbirds, and blackbirds sometimes harass the mighty eagle both on its perch and on the wing. Ordinarily, the eagle manages to ignore them. The adult eagle's visible enemies are few, except for man, because he is the final consumer at the top of his food pyramid.

Fights between individual eagles are uncommon, and this is to the benefit of the species. Intraspecific battles among the birds of prey, equipped as they are for killing, would obviously constitute a threat to the species. Even in winter when the eagles are concentrated around a food supply, they commonly exercise a tolerant indifference toward each other. But not all eagles are alike and, on occasion, hostilities may rise until unusual conflicts ensue.

When eagles are abundant, males sometimes engage in determined aerial battle near their shared territorial borders. The conflict seems to end short of mortal injury. Dr. Milton B. Trautman, while engaged in field studies around the Bass Islands along the western end of Lake Erie, observed two eagles that fought regularly each morning. "These two male eagles would come toward each other from opposite directions," he once told me. "They would fly straight at each other until they came together in mid-air." They clashed each time at some invisible disputed line, and there they fought in futile, daily sessions, perhaps attempting to enforce the ancient rules of territory by which members of the same species divide the available habitat. They rushed at each other, long-curved talons presented, wings fanning the air, and eagle feathers drifting to earth until, at last, exhausted, they would turn their white heads back toward their individual nesting territories. There they would lift themselves on powerful wings to a favorite perch, where they would preen and rearrange their feathers. "Sometimes the fight went on so long," Dr. Trautman recalled, "that we grew tired of watching and left."

Kittens play. Puppies play. Bear cubs play. All the wild subhuman primates play. Colts and calves run and jump, and raccoons tumble and wrestle. Examples of play from the world of birds, however, are far less common and little known. There can, however, be no question that eagles engage in play at various stages in their lives. Young developing eaglets spend 10 weeks or more on the broad platforms where they hatch, and as they grow older they often engage in simple games that involve some "toy" such as a stick or a patch of fur from a rabbit.

Scientists studying eagles at their nests have reported observing the young eagles at play with leaves, sticks, and remnants of food. They may spar and peck at each other, spending their abundant energy. They may use a scrap of flesh or piece of bone from their prey for a game of tug-of-war. Or they may pick up feathers, a cluster of dry leaves, or a stick, and toss them about. Such play has its obvious similarities to acts involved in the capture of food and the defense of territory, indicating a survival value in play.[10]

This youthful play, spawned of abundant energy and stimulated by some external factor, such as a stick or tuft of grass, has seldom been reported to last over into the eagle's adult life, but Dr. Trautman found that adult eagles too engage in games. He tells of observing bald eagles assembled during their migration period on the ice on Buckeye Lake: "Upon two occasions, 3 to 6 eagles were observed playing with a stick. Such a habit appears to be not well known. . . . While standing on Sellars Point in the rather warm, sunny afternoon of February 15, 1930, I watched 6 of these great hawks playing with a stick."

In the beginning of the game the birds, already traveling northward in their spring migration, were grouped about a hole in the ice. Their "toy" was 18 inches long and 1 ½ inches in diameter. First, one of the eagles would take the stick and, lifting itself from the ice, ascend into the sky followed by two or three of the others "in a great circle until it attained a height so great that it could be seen by the naked eye only with difficulty. Thereupon the bird dropped the stick; the others stooped and attempted to catch it with their talons before it hit the ice. The bird catching the stick began to ascend again, screaming all the while, and followed by the others. The game of dropping and recovering the stick continued for more than 10 minutes, after which the birds came down and stood upon the ice about the open hole. During the downward plunges, these usually heavy, awkward hawks appeared surprisingly swift and graceful." Seen in this game is an obvious relationship to the eagle's practice of robbing the osprey, an act by which it garners part of its food supply. But no one can say that what Dr. Trautman witnessed was not play and was not enjoyed by the eagles.[11]

When a bald eagle can find a suitable wind for soaring, it may set its wings and ride the currents, allowing the earth to unroll beneath with no visible effort. Occasionally the eagle's attitude is adjusted by the wing tip primaries, nothing more. The soaring birds sometimes concentrate above a high bank along a lakeshore, as I saw them do one autumn day in northern Minnesota. The winds flowing in off the broad surface of Lake Winnibigoshish were directed skyward by a low cliff. Above the cliff gulls, terns, vultures, red-tailed hawks, and the two neighborhood eagles had flown in to ride these circling, rising winds far into the evening sky, apparently reaping no benefit except the freedom of an effortless ride.

Around the islands of western Lake Erie the eagles some years ago discovered a new way to go soaring. Island Airlines, flying out of Port Clinton in northern Ohio, is one of the world's more unusual airlines. It flies aging, boxlike, Ford Tri-Motor airplanes which, for all their antique appearance, are perfectly suited for those short hops between the mainland and the Bass Islands grouped in the western part of the lake. Dr. Trautman once told me that, while flying on one of these planes from Port Clinton on the Ohio mainland across to Kelly's Island, a distance of 4 miles as the Tri-motor flies, he watched a bald eagle come alongside and position itself near the rear of the wing and slightly above its trailing edge. There the updrafts bouyed it, and the eagle rode the moving air with its wings set, allowing the rumbling old aircraft to pull it along most of the way to the island without the need for a single wingbeat.

Eagles often engage in manificent displays of aerial acrobatics during courtship. The golden eagle, which in some places shares the range of the bald eagle, stages its own spectacular as it plummets from the sky, wings half-folded, closing the distance at speeds of 100 miles an hour or more, until it pulls magnificently out of its dive and sweeps skyward again. Or the two mates, like speeding dark shadows, ride the wild winds, rolling and diving until both are rushing toward each other head-on at fantastic speeds. In the final instant, and with superb timing, one may roll onto its back, pass below its speeding mate, and touch talons with its mate as they pass each other.

The bald eagle has a different routine. As the mating season approaches, the mates become inseparable and the intensity of their nest-building activity reaches its peak. They soar out on the afternoon thermals and rise together so far above the earth that the human eye sees only two distant specks among the clouds. Then, with the rushing winds slipping over their wings, and their bodies under perfect control, the bald eagles sense their power and taste the full excitement of spring. Suddenly one of them rolls over and, flying upside down far above the earth, extends its curved yellow talons in invitation to its mate flying directly above it. With feet extended, the birds touch, their talons intertwine and lock together, and the bird on top rolls over, trading places with its mate; they then cartwheel on set wings over and over toward the earth. Up and over they pinwheel down the spring sky until it seems they will crash to earth. But then they break apart and, on heavy wings, lift themselves away to the security of the eagle's sky again.[12]

4

The Eyrie

THE eagle soaring against the sky seems free. As free as the clouds, the winds, the fog drifting across the lake. Yet, in reality, the eagle is not free at all, except perhaps when young and not yet anchored to mate or eyrie.

For the rest of its life, if it succeeds in entering the breeding population, the eagle lives in bondage, not to the mate, but to the master of both, the territory and particularly the giant treetop nest to which it has become a lifelong caretaker. Wherever the eagle travels, its home territory exerts a magnetic force drawing it back. The eagle's freedoms become little freedoms. It may chose the perch on which it rests, the food it pursues, the hour when it hunts, but it does not escape the demands of the eyrie. The choice is not its own.

The life of the eyrie may span the decades. If an eagle's mate dies, the survivor, still tied to the home territory, is driven to travel beyond the distant hills, rivers, and lakes, searching for a new mate.

The old nest becomes, in turn, master of the latest arrival. Then if its mate should die, it may in turn depart in search of a mate and, with good fortune, bring another strange eagle to share the nest which neither of them built but both will repair, maintain, and use as long as they or the nest remains. In this way the eagle's nest spans the generations. Such was the rule of the eagle's world when the birds had only to contend with natural forces, and before man began disrupting the pattern, destroying the trees, disturbing the birds by crowding into their wilderness, or killing them outright in a variety of ways.[1]

This nest which claims the devotion of the eagle pair in residence is a remarkable structure. Typically, the eagles select for their nest tree a forest giant, a vigorous living plant shaped somewhere near its crown into a fork of at least three limbs. Eagles in search of a tree depend on what is available, red pine in Minnesota, slash pine in Florida, cottonwood, sycamore, shagbark hickory, oak, or cypress. Size, shape, and nearby sources of abundant food seem more important than the species of the tree.

Eagles selecting a nest tree are also influenced by their proximity to other eagles, as the birds have a strong sense of territory. Males will fight to protect the integrity of their territorial borders around the nest even though their hunting grounds may overlap. Within Alaska's Kodiak National Wildlife Refuge wildlife biologists Richard J. Hensel and Willard A. Troyer found nesting pairs of bald eagles defending territories that averaged 57 acres each. The nests of bald eagles, even in the finest eagle country, are widely spaced, and seldom found closer together than one for each mile of shoreline. This can vary, however, and nests surrounded by abundant food supplies have been observed two to the mile along Alaskan coasts, and as many as three to the mile in Florida.[2]

Where no tall tree can be found, the eagle may settle for some less lofty homesite. Charles L. Broley, studying eagles in Florida, found successful nests in the black mangroves 15 feet above the ground. On rare occasions bald eagles have been found nesting on cliffside ledges after the manner of their cousins, the golden eagles.

On Amchitka, the Aleutian island famous for sea otters, eagles, and atomic tests, there are no trees, so the eagles must build their nests on the ground in situations completely foreign to mainland eagles. Centuries of wave action have cut at the lava cliffs until tall columns of black rock stand in isolated pinnacles with their bases in the water at high tide. I have seen these intertidal sea stacks standing perhaps 40 feet high, and topped with a tuft of coarse, thick grass fitted like a shaggy green wig. Only birds reach this luxuriant little green meadow, and a pair of bald eagles can live there in full command, their nest covering most of the top of the column, safer from a climber than a tree nest would be.

Olaus J. Murie, who first went to the Aleutians in 1936 to study the wildlife for the United States Biological Survey, later the Fish and Wildlife Service, found that one such ancient nest, 6 feet deep, was a crypt layered with the bones of shearwaters, fulmars, puffins, and other seabirds, the eagles' major food in the Aleutians. There are not, however, enough of these stone columns to serve all the breeding pairs of eagles on Amchitka, and those who possess no such rocky spire must build their nests at ground level on the edge of the cliff that overlooks the sea.[3]

Although circumstances may force sea eagles to nest

in low places, the towering tree seems the universal preference. Once a pair has chosen its nest tree, the work pro-
gresses hour after hour, daylight to dark, for about four
days. Into the tree the birds ferry a wide variety of materials. They may bring sticks 6 feet long and branches 2 inches
in diameter. Occasionally they vary the material with pieces
of sod, corn stalks, moss, or weeds. The materials they
gather are usually picked up from the ground as the eagle
swoops low and lifts its stick without landing. But on occasion the nest-building eagle sees an attractive branch still
attached to a tree and, flying at high speed, extends its feet,
cracks and breaks the limb from the tree, and flies off trium-
phantly with it to its nest.

The sticks placed upon the nest are arranged with the
bill into a platform about 2 feet deep and 5 or more feet
across. This is the basic structure. Then the eagles gather
grass for a mattress by flying low over the surrounding
fields, pulling tufts of dry brown vegetation with their talons as they pass, then flying off to their tree trailing long
brown streamers behind them.

At last only one thing remains to complete the job.
One of the pair must bring to the nest a sprig of fresh
greenery. White pine is a favorite. It is carried home and
placed in the nest as if for decoration. No human can say
why this custom prevails among the bald eagles, and some
other birds of prey as well, or whether or not it has any
practical value to the birds. But as climber Jack Stewart told
me, "The evergreen branch is always there."

As the mating season approaches, the eagles are
driven with a growing urgency to repair the old nest for the

new year. Around the Great Lakes this may begin as early as February, as the eagles swoop lower over the earth to pick up new supplies of sticks and grass. These building materials are arranged on the old nest, sometimes adding a foot or more to its depth.

The eagle's nest may contain more than sticks and grass. Nests checked in Florida were found to include a Clorox bottle, a long white candle, an electric light bulb, an old shoe, a family portrait (framed), and a pair of pink panties.[4]

The home of the eagle becomes a refuge for smaller creatures as well. Songbirds often pause on the edge of eagle nests, a few feet from the nesting bird. One morning while I photographed a pair of eagles at their nest in Minnesota, a Baltimore oriole came to the edge of the nest at dawn, when both adult eagles and their young were there. The oriole paused to sing, hopped to a branch adjoining the nest, and finally flew off. At least two other small birds visited the nest that morning.

John B. Holt, a nimble and able climber who has worked with Sergej Postupalsky in his banding of Michigan eagles for many years, once told me he had found a porcupine in an eagle's nest: "It had made itself a den in the lower part of the structure. It was lying in there when I went up to get into the nest. We tried to ignore each other."

Even snakes may go up on occasion and take shelter within the eagle's castle. One day, when far above the ground in the top of a pine tree, the famed eagle bander Charles Broley heard a "loud reptilian hissing," then found himself eye to eye with a large coachwhip snake, harmless except perhaps when encountered by surprise in the top of a tree. There was no question that the snake was a longtime resident, as several of its cast-off skins decorated the eagle's nest.

An eagle that leaves its territory for the winter may return early in spring to find that the nest has meanwhile become the sleeping quarters of a raccoon, which, given the opportunity, would speedily devour the eagle's unguarded eggs. The presence of the raccoon may prompt the eagles to move to another tree and build an alternate nest.

Likewise in winter the great horned owl, surveying the forest for a nest site, is often tempted by the eagle's nest, especially if the eagles are still away. By early spring, when the eagles return, the owls may be in firm possession, perhaps with young owls already prospering in the nursery intended for eagles. Instead of engaging in battle and attempting to evict the invaders, the eagles often move on.

There have, however, been rare instances in which neither eagle nor owl was willing to give up, and they adjusted to uneasy double occupancy, with the eagle sitting on top of the nest and the uninvited guest incubating its eggs in a crude hollow somewhere below. Stranger still was Charles Broley's 1939 experience in Florida: "I found a Great Horned Owl incubating one of its own eggs and one of a bald eagle. The eagle egg was in good condition, but unfortunately the tree was cut before the eggs hatched."[5]

It is common for a pair of eagles to have more than one nest within the territory and use them alternately. If they return in the spring, already driven by the urgency of the new nesting cycle, to find their favorite tree destroyed by a storm, they can quickly turn to a spare nest and recondition it for early occupancy.

Nesting must begin early in the spring through most of the eagle's range, leaving time enough to rear the young and see them fledged and capable of doing their own hunting before the test of winter. The schedule is tight for large birds. There is so little time. If the first clutch of eggs fails to hatch, nesting is abandoned for the year, and if a nest is blown down, even early in the season, the birds get nothing accomplished during the year except to rebuild their nest, leaving it ready but empty until the following spring.

For Florida eagles, nesting activity begins not in spring but in autumn. The old birds are already repairing their nests by September or October, eggs are incubating by November or December, and the young are being fed in January and February. One reason often mentioned is the weather. As William Meiners and Morlan Nelson have observed of the golden eagle: "It is a known fact that all eyries with southern exposure and no shade from the afternoon sun are hazardous to young birds. Direct rays of the sun from 2:00 to 5:00 when the temperature reaches 96 degrees are lethal to the eaglets."[6] In the summer of 1970 eyries in Idaho exposed to direct sunlight had become deathbeds for eight young eagles found by Nelson. Bald eagles, equally vulnerable, live in treetop nests normally exposed to the sun, and their protection on those blistering midsummer afternoons must come from the shade of their parents, hovering over them with half-extended wings. If the old birds are frightened and kept away from the nest tree, as they sometimes have been by the endless stream of visitors and bird watchers, the young may not make it through the day. Young eagles hatched in Florida during the winter are already protected by a covering of insulating feathers when summer brings the searing subtropical sun.

For all its reputation as a bird of fierce nature and frightening temperament, the bald eagle, even on the nest and in charge of its eggs, is normally docile and easily frightened away by people. Exceptions are notable and sometimes dramatic, as in the case of the eagle that chased a helicopter. During a survey of bald eagle nests around Chesapeake Bay in 1962, the helicopter in which the eagle watchers were traveling came clattering toward the nest where a bald eagle guarded a single chick. When the helicopter was 100 yards away, the eagle left the nest in swift pursuit and swooped directly at the machine. It repeated its attacks several times, forcing the pilot to employ evasive tactics to keep the eagle from striking the rotors and causing a crash. The eagle pursued the machine for half a mile in her successful efforts to chase it away from her eyrie.[7]

One day the female crouches on her nest for perhaps an hour; then she stands and, turning her head sideways, looks down at a new egg, warm and moist. Incubation begins soon afterwards, but in the following days she will usually lay a second egg, and sometimes a third.

The egg of the bald eagle is usually white, or nearly so, plain and without markings. It is thick and bluntly rounded on the ends. The eagle's egg is only slightly larger than the egg of the chicken—rather small for such a large bird. During perhaps 40 days of incubation, both parents share the work of warming the eggs. While one mate occupies the nest, the other is off hunting or standing guard on a prominent nearby perch.

Breaking out of the shell is not a simple task. The strength of the shell resists the force and weight of the blind and struggling eaglet chipping away at the inner surface to free itself. Dr. Francis Herrick was an eyewitness to this process. In 1931 he obtained a clutch of fertile bald eagle eggs from Canada and hatched them beneath a domestic hen. At last, late one afternoon, he stood in his laboratory holding a warm hatching egg in the palm of his hand. In those final hours of imprisonment, as the eaglet chipped away at the shell with its egg tooth, Dr. Herrick's scientific training told him not to help the young one escape. His role was that of observer. But the struggle of the eaglet in those critical hours caused a certain erosion of scientific discipline. Dr. Herrick admitted later that "this eaglet was given aid in piercing its shell, and the opening was somewhat enlarged to insure the bird free access to the air."[8]

If the eggs are destroyed in the early days of incubation, or taken from the nest, the old bird may later produce a second clutch. But if the nest is destroyed, or the young lost, the nesting efforts cease for the entire year. When young are in the nest and both parents are needed to share the hunting and nest guarding, the loss of one of the adults is a tragedy of staggering proportions. Under these circumstances unattached birds of prey have been observed, on rare occasions, to adopt the young of others of their kind.[9]

There is a family of eagles in Michigan which nests on the private grounds of a hunt club whose members jealously guard their safety. One day the caretaker reported that the female, known by her larger size, had vanished. She was perhaps the adult bald eagle whose body was later discovered floating in a nearby lake. Suddenly the male was left alone both to hunt for food and to guard the young. Eaglebander Jack Holt told me a few years later how the problem was resolved. "In addition to the old birds," he said, "there had been an immature eagle hanging around and I figured by its size that it might be a female. Shortly after the old female disappeared, this young bird, which might have been only two or three years old at the time, joined the old male at the nest. She took up the dead female's duties and they raised those young ones."

Birds of prey begin their incubation when the first egg is laid, and for this reason the young within the nest may vary in size. The first hatched chick is already well started when the second one arrives and will have first choice of the food delivered by the parents, sometimes leaving the smaller bird to go hungry.

All young eagles in high places live close to the elements and face frequent hazards. The older an eagle nest becomes, the larger it may grow. The largest bald eagle nests on record have been about 20 feet deep. The famous one at Vermilion, Ohio, was known to have been occupied for 36 years without interruption. It attained an estimated weight of 2 tons, measured 12 feet high and 8½ feet across. A nest measured in Florida was larger still, 9½ feet wide and 20 feet deep, perhaps the largest eagle nest of record.[10]

Eventually the size and growing weight of the massive nest become a threat to the tree and to the birds that use it. The eagle tree, old and megacephalic, finds its burden growing heavier as its own ability to withstand the added weight diminishes. The giant misshapen head, the foreign growth in its crown, now dominates the tree. The weight of sticks and moist decaying humus become a malignancy. The cells of the tree die, the fibers weakening with advancing age, and yet, year after year, the eagle pair returns to carry more sticks to its endangered eyrie.

Then on a dark night in early spring the storm arrives. Whitecaps pattern the rolling surface of the black water, while the rushing winds test every object they meet. At the height of the storm, when the blackened sky is marked with jagged streaks of white fire and the world rocks to the rolling and crashing thunder, the relentless winds gather new strength and seem to concentrate their power on a target that has resisted them perhaps for three centuries. The old tree groans and bends, then bends too far, and from somewhere within its brittle form comes the sound of cracking and breaking wood that rises above the howling of the wind. The forest giant, shuddering and trembling, has leaned with the winds before, and stood. But on this night it dies. The giant, soggy nest of rain-soaked sticks it has borne so long leans crazily, hesitates for a moment, then tumbles end-over-end out of the falling tree more than 80 feet straight down to the earth. There it lies, a heap of organic matter, to decay and vanish as it feeds the decomposers. Somewhere in or around the heap of sticks and humus may be the eagles' eggs and their hope for the year.

If any young were in the nest, their fate is determined by the nature of the place into which they fall, the temperament of their parents, and how close they may be to an age where they can fly and begin caring for themselves. Postupalsky and Holt reported the case of a tree in which they had banded two young eagles. A week after the climb the Michigan countryside was swept by a raging storm, and the two eagle men, concerned about the young eagles in the aging tree, pushed through miles of underbrush and swamp to check on them. Where the tree had once stood there was now only open blue sky. The fall had scattered the eagle's nest, killing one of the young birds. The other still sat on the nest materials, emaciated and abandoned in the thick brush where the parent birds could not easily have flown to feed it. The eagle men shipped the chick to the Patuxent Wildlife Research Center in Maryland to serve as a subject for scientists working on the problems of the endangered national bird.

Somewhat happier was the ending of a disaster at an eagle's nest during the summer of 1960 in Sandusky County, on a farm along the south shore of Lake Erie. The owner of the farm had watched from his fields all spring and summer as a pair of old eagles attended to their duties. Then one morning following a storm he found one of the young birds on the ground. He went to the house at once and called Laurel Van Camp, the county game protector, who related the story to me.

They soon found another nestling on the ground. They hauled out some snow fence and built a large pen around the young eagles to keep out dogs and other predators. The parents began at once to deliver food to their two grounded chicks, coming in from the lake and the beaches with fish. The young eagles gained strength and soon joined their parents in the sky.

Meanwhile, high above the ground, a tragedy had occurred. The old eagles, busy with the two grounded chicks, had neglected a third that had not fallen from the nest.

5

The Eagles of Vermilion

THE Lake Shore Railroad stretched along the southern edge of Lake Erie, past the woodlots and rolling farm country, through the sleepy villages, and sometimes within sight of the giant lake to the north. Aboard the rumbling train one September day in 1899 was Dr. Francis H. Herrick, a neatly dressed professor of zoology returning from the east to his home in Cleveland. As naturalists might be expected to do, Dr. Herrick spent much of his time watching from the window, studying the landscape for glimpses of wildlife.

Shortly after the train rolled across the border into Ohio, as Dr. Herrick sat looking out over Lake Erie, he saw a majestic adult bald eagle. It traveled in a straight course toward a massive nest in plain view at the top of a giant sycamore. Dr. Herrick removed a small notebook from his jacket and wrote down the location of the nest, promising himself that, when spring returned, he would come back for a closer look at these birds and their eyrie.

Dr. Herrick, a noted authority on the life of the lobster, had recently become head of the Department of Biology at Western Reserve University. There was nothing particularly unusual about switching from lobsters to eagles. Naturalists were generalists, interested in all kinds of wildlife, and anywhere a naturalist looked there were exciting questions yet to be answered. If eagles should attract his attention, this was reason enough for the scholarly Dr. Herrick to study them.

One day the following summer, when the eagle family should have been secure and prospering in the crown of the sycamore, Dr. Herrick returned to the nest he had seen from his speeding train, but the nest was no longer perched on its sycamore pillar. During the winter, a storm had sent it tumbling to the ground, where he found the remains, scattered among the broken dead branches of the sycamore.[1]

Dr. Herrick soon found the eagles' new nest, also in a sycamore, a few hundred yards to the east of the fallen tree. This nest was a shallow bowl of gray sticks. But Dr. Herrick was frustrated: The bald eagle, by building its huge nest as close to the sky as possible, had made it inaccessible to close scrutiny. Such elevations prevented even the most vigorous naturalists from studying the secrets of the eagle's family life. Dr. Herrick began scheming how to interject himself into the hidden world of the baby eagle and record the daily activities there with his cameras. This was a challenge that would take him to one eagle's nest after another through the following years and to the tops of the tallest trees along the south shore of Lake Erie. He began planning a tower that would lift him to the level of the eagles.

But one project gets in the way of another. Old jobs, not quite completed, must go on; students and studies demand a professor's time. Two decades passed before Dr. Herrick returned to his plan to build a tower to the eagles. In the autumn of 1921 he drove with a friend to see an eagle's nest beside the shore of Lake Erie near Vermilion, Ohio, west of Cleveland. Nowhere in the annals of science was there a record of a nest larger or grander than this Vermilion structure.

By asking questions around the community Dr. Herrick learned that the nest had been occupied, perhaps continuously, for 31 years. Older residents could recall eagle nests in the community or point to records extending back fully 90 years to 1830. Ancestors of the eagles he found at Vermilion had lived on these shores and heard the first broad axes ring in the hardwood forests.[2]

The nest had grown a layer at a time over the years until it was 12 feet deep, a huge cone of interlocked sticks and rotting humus supported in the lofty crotch of a giant shellbark hickory. Its surface was a platform 8½ feet across, a playground for baby eagles. Dr. Herrick estimated the weight of the great nest at 2 tons and worried at times about the ability of the aging tree to support its growing weight. But for the moment the tree looked equal to its burden, so Dr. Herrick hurried to complete plans for his eagle observatory.

Eighty-five feet south of the eagle tree there was a

giant elm. During the winter of 1921–22 Dr. Herrick's crew of workmen built a ladder into the top of the elm tree. There, 82 feet above the earth, they constructed a platform, working rapidly to finish before the eagles would return to their nest in the late winter. The platform was equipped with a tent, claimed by Dr. Herrick to be the first tent-type blind used for bird photography. By working inside the tent, photographing the birds through a small window, Herrick could hide his movements from the powerful eyes of the eagles. Looking down from his new platform, the elated observer, after years of waiting, enjoyed an unparalleled view of the national bird in its home.

This high-rise perch turned out to be only the first of several structures used by Dr. Herrick for eagle watching, as a series of misfortunes plagued his efforts. That first platform was 9 feet square and equipped with a railing around the tent. Ropes and wires helped secure the platform against the gales that sometimes howled in off the lake. To reach the blind the eagle watchers climbed a steel ladder straight up the side of the tree, then entered the tent through a small trap door in the bottom of the platform. Dr. Herrick was still not satisfied. The following year he added a second story to the tower, and this took him 30 feet higher. Perched at this dizzying height he looked down happily upon the nesting eagles throughout the long weeks of summer.

Until now, the Vermilion eagles had lived for years familiar to the local farmers and townsfolk but largely ignored. People saw the big birds soaring off over the lake or circling the woods where they nested, but the eagles were simply part of the scene as they always had been. Dr. Herrick worried, as the crew began building the tree house, that these strange activities would draw the curious into the area and that people would disturb the eagles and climb the tower. "Our fears in this direction," he said later, "were fully justified, for the Vermilion eagles, who had hitherto pursued the even tenor of their lives with little molestation, suddenly entered upon a fame not all to their liking." As the Vermilion eagles became nationally famous, sightseers began arriving from distant places. These uninvited visitors seldom understood that the eagles would not be active when there were people in the vicinity, or that there was little they might actually see except the bottom of the platform perched in the top of an elm tree.[3]

Disaster stalked the project. The eggs failed to hatch the first year, and the second year one of the eagle pair was shot. Then, during the winter of 1925–26, Dr. Herrick began construction of a steel tower similar to those used by forest fire watchers. The structure rose to 80 feet. Its steel legs were solidly set in concrete, and the eagle watchers worked with a new confidence in their structure. The prized tower was still bright and new when a May storm rumbled in across the lakeshore. The tower withstood the onslaught beautifully, but the eagle tree snapped off cleanly just below the giant nest. Tons of limbs and old nesting materials crashed to earth carrying along three half-grown eaglets that had been under almost daily observation.

Later that year the frustrated professor rounded up his Western Reserve University construction crew again and had the tower moved 80 miles to the east, beside still another eagle nest. The following spring the tower was used for several weeks of spying on the new pair of eagles.

But the two eggs failed to hatch and finally, on April 27, were destroyed, perhaps by the unsuccessful parents. Winter came. Again the eagle tower was carefully taken down, loaded onto trucks and hauled back to Vermilion, where the old familiar pair of eagles had constructed a new nest, higher than ever. Dr. Herrick's steel structure rose up beside this nest until it towered 91 feet above the earth and contained more than four tons of steel. Inside the blind, Dr. Herrick looked down into the gigantic nest from a distance of only 38 feet.

Perhaps, in time, earthbound man becomes accustomed to climbing into the sky and perching there while strong winds sway him back and forth against the clouds. There is security to be felt in the strength of the steel, as you look down upon the tallest forest trees and watch the crawling trains and lake boats moving across the scene below. Dr. Herrick ascended the ladder each day, convinced that it could withstand the forces of nature. There was no way he could have forecast the onslaught of the two-day storm of early May, 1929. Out of the northeast came winds so violent that small creatures were driven to earth. For hour on hour the punishing winds beat against the eagle nest and the tower. The nest came through without loss, but Dr. Herrick's tower was torn from its concrete moorings and toppled to earth.

On the heels of the storm the undaunted professor set about erecting an even taller tower, a 96-foot giant. Soon his cameras, binoculars, and notebooks were once more in use. Dr. Herrick and his co-workers continued to study every movement of the giant birds until eventually, more than a quarter of a century after the plan first occurred to him, he completed his historic study of the bald eagle. Dr. Herrick had watched through his cameras and binoculars for hundreds of hours and written in his notebooks the detailed schedules of the eagles' daily activities. This approach can no longer be easily practiced, because eagles are rare now and the areas around those nests still active are properly protected from invasions that might disturb the birds and reduce the possibilities that their eggs will hatch.

In recent times towers have been used more often by photographers than by research scientists. Karl H. Maslowski built such a tower in northern Ohio in 1962 to obtain movies of the bald eagles nesting on the Winous Point Club grounds. Maslowski tells me there was a single eaglet in the nest and that, unlike most baby eagles, it had a human name. "We called it Francis," he said, "in honor of Dr. Herrick." Young Francis may have descended from one of the eagles Dr. Herrick studied forty years before, not many miles to the east.

The nest tree at Winous Point was an American elm suffering from Dutch elm disease. The following year the tree was dead, and the bark was slipping and peeling from its trunk and limbs; the eagles moved to a new tree a mile away. The old tree with its abandoned nest stood until November 22, 1963.

In northern Ohio on that day, waterfowl biologist John M. Anderson, then manager of the Winous Point Club, and later director of the sanctuary program for the National Audubon Society, drove out the long, twisting lane to his mail box. As he passed the old elm tree he glanced up by habit, and noted that the familiar eagle nest was still there. While he was at the mail box, his car radio brought the first news of the shooting of the president. Gripped by the sense of shock that struck most Americans in that hour, Anderson drove slowly back along the lane toward his home. Almost by reflex he glanced into the eagle tree. "The eagle nest," he said later, "had fallen from the tree and crashed to the ground in the same hour that President Kennedy was shot."

Few people around Vermilion, Ohio, today recall the eagles and "the great nest" that first attracted Dr. Herrick. I stopped on a recent summer afternoon and visited the small lakeside museum maintained there by the Great Lakes Historical Society. The schoolgirl attending the information desk knew nothing of eagles or even of local people who might be interested in birds. "Why don't you ask Mr. Copeland," she suggested hopefully, and out of the corner came A. D. Copeland.

"I heard just enough," he volunteered, "to spark my interest. I remember those eagles. Used to lie on the ground under that nest when I was a boy and watch them through my telescope. The nest was on the farm where my aunt lived. After the nest fell, the eagles moved about two miles to the old Hahn Farm. Somebody shot one of the eagles once and people almost ran him out of town."

The month of the eagle's shooting was November 1924. The body was preserved by the Cleveland Museum of Natural History, which Dr. Herrick had helped found, and the following year, at the request of the governor of Ohio, the mounted eagle became the center of a display viewed by thousands of people attending the state fair in Columbus. This eagle can still be seen in the Cleveland Museum.

Vermilion, once a sleepy lakeside village with room for eagles, has prospered as the years passed. Its population of 1,500 has grown to 10,000, and the land where the Vermilion eagles once lived in a tree is now the site of a giant, sprawling industrial complex, assembling automobiles—which are shipped off on the same railroad Dr. Herrick once traveled coming out from Cleveland to watch the eagles. "No," said Mr. Copeland, "I don't remember Dr. Herrick, but I recall the eagles very well. Used to watch them for hours."

6

A Matter of Diet

BECAUSE of what they eat, or are believed to eat, eagles have been persecuted over the centuries by men determined to save their domestic animals and children. Automatically, large predators have been classified as enemies of man, to be feared, reviled, and eliminated. Eagles have ranked close behind the wolves as predators with which men must contend.

But the food of the eagle is that of an opportunist taking what it can when it cannot find what it prefers. One way to learn what the eagle really eats is to go to its eyrie to find and identify the remains of the victims.

When the great nest at Vermilion crashed during the spring of 1925, the bald eagles there had been under attack by farmers accusing the eagles of taking turkeys, ducks, chickens, lambs and various other domestic creatures. These stories had been told and retold, and the alleged crimes of the Vermilion eagles had politicians, farmers, conservation organizations, and even school children choosing sides. From the state capitol in Columbus came orders for employees of the Ohio Fish and Game Commission to investigate the eagles, learn what the birds were eating, and determine if, as some argued, they should be killed.

By this time the youthful and scrappy Izaak Walton League of America had waded into the argument on behalf of the Vermilion eagles. Along with others, the IWL suggested that instead of destroying the eagles, a fund be set up to reimburse the farmers for actual losses. Dr. Herrick and his coworkers, through long weeks in their treetop blinds, had carefully observed the food habits of the accused, watching them return to the nest on trip after trip. Dr. Herrick's calculations showed the Vermilion eagles' diet to be at least 70 percent fish in 1922 and a full 96 percent fish in 1923.[1]

During the winter of 1924–25 nothing was done toward reaching a final conclusion. The controversy flared up now and then but for the most part lay dormant. Finally, the elements contributed hard evidence in defense of the threatened birds. The ancient shellbark hickory whose limbs had been dying as it supported the growing weight of the giant nest finally toppled on the evening of March 10, 1925. Dr. Herrick realized at once that he had been handed abundant raw materials to provide clues on the diet of the Vermilion eagles. Over the years the finer particles of decaying wood, earth, feathers, fur, and bone within the nest had sifted down through the top layers of sticks to form a mass of loamy organic material in the heart of the eagle's lodge. Within this tomb were the bones and feathers of uncounted smaller creatures that had nourished the generations of great white-headed eagles and their young. Because this mass of organic matter had a frozen core when the nest fell, the fall failed to destroy the nest or scatter it widely. Dr. Herrick and his assistants began the tedious but challenging chore of separating and identifying the nest materials.

As they anticipated, fish predominated. Fish bones were mixed with those of domestic chickens and various wild birds. There were also remains of crows, grebes, plovers, and even one young eagle. There was identifiable evidence of rabbits, muskrats, rats, and squirrels. But the percentage of domestic poultry was small, and nowhere was there evidence that the Vermilion eagles had carried off lamb, pig, or calf.

Almost certainly the largest of eagles could not lift some of the creatures they have been accused of taking, and this includes children. Time and knowledge begin to erase prejudice and temper fiction. Somewhere in my youth I saw a book with a dramatic illustration showing a child being borne off among the clouds in the talons of a mighty, frowning eagle. The plump victim, all purity and innocence, garbed in a snow-white dress, was obviously, and understandably, in fear for her life. The eagle, looking fierce and all-powerful, appeared to carry its human burden without effort. After nearly half a century I recall that picture and nothing else from the book. Not until years later did I begin to understand its basic fiction, or learn that there is only one case on record of a bald eagle attacking a baby, and this one usually discounted. The instance was recorded in 1832, and the eagle was said to have torn away part of the infant's dress in a vain effort to lift it.[2]

Such stories force us to consider the lifting power of

this bird of prey. How much weight a 10- or 12-pound eagle can carry is not easily determined with precision techniques. The lifting ability of one wild golden eagle was tested in Texas in the spring of 1937 by attaching weights to the eagle's feet and turning it free. The eagle weighed 11 pounds. But, burdened with weight of 5¼ pounds, it was helpless when trying to lift itself into the air. In California a few years later another eagle, carrying 8 pounds of dead weight, was released from a 15-foot platform only to struggle along about 12 yards before being pulled to earth by the burden. The factors that determine the ability of an eagle to lift and carry weight include direction and speed of wind, physical condition of the bird, and how badly it wants to lift the weight. But the conclusion of Dr. Richard R. Olendorff, after conducting research at Colorado State University, is that the golden eagle flying with 7 or 8 pounds of weight "approaches the upper limit even in wind-aided situations."[3]

Eagles do not have to lift everything on which they feed. They have undoubtedly killed, on occasion, creatures too large for them to carry. There are even examples of eagles attacking full-grown antelope or deer, sometimes successfully. But the bald eagle does not go about wildly chasing cattle, deer, antelope, or even sheep. Such large creatures normally pay the passing eagle not even slight attention unless they are guarding young. The foods of the eagle are smaller creatures: they are known to kill turtles, birds (such as ducks) and small mammals (such as rabbits), but where there is a preference the bald eagle chooses fish for its meal. This fact binds it to the water, and makes it a citizen of the seacoasts, rivers, and lake shores. Nor is the eagle a purist after the manner of the human angler, equipped with perfect fly rod, demanding that his fish leap and splash. Dead fish floating belly-up are perfectly acceptable to the bald eagle and far easier to reduce to possession. For this reason the eagle off on a daybreak hunting trip may first fly at high altitude over the lake scanning the dark waters for the fish that did not make it through the night. A distant white spot on the water determines the bird's course. It descends swiftly to the target, dips one talon into the water, clasps the fish, and carries it off toward the eyrie without pause.

On days when scavenging and fishing are poor some eagles turn to robbery and keep a sharp eye upon the osprey. Some years ago, when eagles and ospreys were more common, I watched this dramatic competition above Orange Lake in central Florida. It is an unforgettable contest. A boat sits motionless at midday on a placid lake. Nothing moves. No wind, no fish. The relentless heat of the summer sun silences all creatures. The fisherman dozes. Then from somewhere behind him comes the startling crash of a body hitting the water, the splash of perhaps a large leaping bass. But it is not a fish. Instead, it is an osprey struggling now to rise from the lake with a 2-pound fish gripped in its talons.

Other eyes have noticed, and flying swiftly toward the center of the lake from the towering cypress trees along the eastern shore is a bald eagle, pushing for top speed. Winging in from above, the eagle swoops upon the smaller bird as if to strike the burdened osprey between its shoulders. The osprey dodges and refuses to drop the fish while the eagle banks, gains altitude, and comes down upon it a second time. Twice more the eagle swoops upon the osprey until at last the osprey drops its fish and flies safely away. The fish tumbles 200 feet to splash hard against the surface while behind it the eagle swoops on half-folded wings, plummeting toward the dark water in a vain effort to overtake the falling fish. There is an instant when the eagle might pick the fish from the water, but the fish is too far ahead of the eagle and vanishes quickly into the water, leaving both osprey and eagle hungry.

There are variations. A resourceful eagle has been seen to fly in beneath the osprey that fails to release its fish, turn onto its back, and reach up with those fearsome talons to pull the fish by force from the bird that captured it. But these views are rare. In those scarce and scattered locations where eagles still live, there are seldom osprey to rob, because the osprey, like the eagle, is vanishing from the wild scene.

From his treetop tower Dr. Herrick repeatedly watched the Vermilion eagles leave the nest to fly out over Lake Erie until eventually they were lost from view. Then an eagle would return, first as a dot on the horizon, then growing steadily larger until even the struggling fish was visible securely trapped in the iron grip of the talons. Dr. Herrick regretfully admitted that he never witnessed a fishing eagle striking the water. His movies of the flying eagles, however, revealed that half or more of the fish carried to the nest "were undoubtedly taken alive."[4]

Along the spruce-lined bays of southeast Alaska, biologist Fred Robards has often watched eagles dive into the water, sometimes disappearing completely beneath the surface. Usually they reappear carrying a fish in their talons. Sometimes an eagle miscalculates and attacks a fish too large to handle. "The eagle doesn't give up and release the fish," Robards told me, "but just hangs onto it and starts to swim toward shore." The swimming eagle is robbed of its grace, especially if it has a fish in tow. Clumsily it beats its wings upon the water, gradually pulling itself shoreward.

Eagles will also dive into the water on occasion when attempting to capture ducks or coots. Each day, when hungry, the eagle may perch in a tree above the pool where the coots gather to feed. As John W. Baker described it in 1881: "At the first sight of the eagle the coots all huddled together. There they swam about nervously, casting uneasy glances up in the direction of their enemy."[5]

Finally the eagle, ready to make his move, lifts himself from the perch. Frantically the coots press together in a solid dark raft, a blanket of birds upon the pond. But their nerve does not hold. The giant bird of prey drops on speeding wings; as it does, the coots rise as one in a thunderous noise, beating the water with feet and wingtips, struggling to gain speed and clear the water to safety. This is not what the eagle wants. He cannot strike an entire flock of coots, so he dives upon the frantic birds time and again until eventually one is cut from the flock. Now the eagle shifts its attention from the flock to concentrate on the lone coot.

But the dumpy blue-gray victim begins diving to escape the death promised by those long curved talons. Finally the frustrated eagle plunges into the water behind the coot. Time passes, and it begins to seem that the great eagle has drowned. But it reappears at last, the coot firmly gripped in its talons. The weary eagle lifts from the water and struggles to a low limb to rest before eating its hard-won prey.

In Glacier Bay National Monument the favorite perch of one bald eagle, a long-time resident, was in a tall spruce tree in front of the park supervisor's home. "When he was not hungry," the supervisor once told me, "this is where he would come to rest, and while he sat there he would ignore everything around him, including the small birds even if they actually struck him." This imperturbable eagle had a special hunting technique. Noting where the ducks drifted near the edge of the bay, he would fly off across the forest. Then he would return, flying at high speed at treetop level, hidden by the screen of trees. Coming to the edge of the forest at full speed, he half-folded his wings and plummeted down upon the scattering ducks, a technique that worked for the eagle about one time out of four.

Ducks are appealing enough to an eagle that they can sometimes lure the giant predators away from their nests. Marine biologist Karl Kenyon, while working in the Aleutian Islands for the United States Bureau of Sport Fisheries and Wildlife, watched a pair of mallards lead a pursuing eagle away from a pond, flying only far enough ahead of the eagle to tease it into pursuit. When they had taken the eagle more than a mile from the nest pond, they turned and left it alone as they circled and backtracked toward their nest.[6]

Alexander Wilson, the earliest of America's bird artists, once recorded a remarkable event witnessed in the early 1800s along the Ohio River. There have been years when thousands of gray squirrels migrate en masse through the summer forests, driven by some mysterious urgency which prompts them to attempt to swim any waters they encounter. Some make it and some drown. "In one of those partial migrations of tree squirrels that sometimes takes place in our western forests," Wilson wrote, "many thousands of them were drowned in attempting to cross the Ohio; and at a certain place, not far from Wheeling, a prodigious number of their dead bodies were floating to the shore by an eddy. Here the vultures assembled in great force, and regaled themselves for some time, when a bald eagle made his appearance, and took sole possession of the premises, keeping the vultures at their proper distance for several days."[7]

In Alaska, where most bald eagles take their food from the edge of the sea, they have been observed to feed on sea urchins and abalone exposed by low tide.

In winter eagles are likely to feed more heavily on adult waterfowl, partly because the fish may be difficult to obtain, and partly because waterfowl may be concentrated and readily available. Eagles around hunting areas frequently feed on ducks and geese crippled or left dead in the field. As Arthur C. Bent reported, however, the eagle "is perfectly capable of catching a duck on the wing and frequently does so. . . . I have seen two eagles chasing a black duck in the air until it was forced down in the water."[8] William Brewster observed eagles capturing brant along the Virginia coast: "The eagle's flight, ordinarily slow and somewhat heavy, becomes, in the excitement of pursuit, exceedingly swift and graceful, and the fugitive is quickly overtaken. When close upon its quarry the eagle suddenly sweeps beneath it, and, turning back downwards, thrusts its powerful talons into its breast."[9]

Young eagles in the nest are fed the food of their parents from their first meals. Their first feedings are delivered by the male, then torn to bite size by the female. The growing chicks, equipped from youth with rugged talons and strong bills, are soon capable of tearing their own food from the bulk portions delivered to the nest.

Food may also be the lure used to tempt the nearly grown eagles to make their maiden flight. The nest is the only world they know, a place where all their needs have been faithfully supplied by their devoted parents. Now they are expected to push themselves from the nest, fly out across the towering treetops over a threatening void where only their wings can keep them from falling. For days they have jumped stiff-legged about the nest, flapping and strengthening their broad wings in miniature, make-believe flights.

Then one of the parents comes in from the lake carrying a tantalizing fish in plain view. The young eagles expect the parent to drop the fish into the nest just as it has hundreds of times before, and they set up a hoarse, screeching welcome. But the parent passes low across the nest flying very slowly. The young bird can stand the temptation no longer. Suddenly one chick is in the air above the nest and the circling mother calls and swoops down before him. The young bird pursues the tempting food with a mounting singleness of purpose. His weeks of practice hops about the nest have prepared him for this hour and he flies along on frantically pounding wings behind his mother for a full mile before she comes to her perch in a tree at the edge of the forest. There she offers her young one its reward.[10]

7

The Champion Eagle Bander

ALL who study the bald eagle owe a lasting debt to Charles L. Broley, the "eagle man." In his "retirement" career as an eagle bander, Broley scaled hundreds of trees. He would swing, spiderlike, on a web of fragile ropes, a hundred feet above the earth, until he could secure a death grip on a jungle of sticks and heave himself into a nest of protesting—and sometimes threatening—birds.

One afternoon in a small office in Washington, D.C., I talked about Broley with Richard H. Pough, the professional conservationist who had first influenced Broley to climb to the eagles. "Charles Broley was a quiet, unassuming person," Pough recalled. "Friendly. People liked him. He was tough and wiry, and he worked every day at staying in shape. During the season when he was climbing he did

twenty push-ups every morning. This is remarkable,"
Pough added, "when you realize that he didn't begin working with eagles until his sixtieth year, when he had retired
from his job."

By profession Broley had been a manager of a branch
bank in Winnipeg, Manitoba. When he retired, in 1938, he
planned, like other retired bankers, to travel, sit in the sun,
play a little shuffleboard, and not much more.He did have
one hobby, however, which had brought him long and wonderful days in the fields and along the sloughs of his native
prairie province: he was intensely interested in birds, especially the hundreds of thousands of ducks and geese that
annually passed through central Manitoba between their
breeding and wintering areas. He knew the waterfowl and
the shorebirds, and the most exciting days he could recall
were those when he and his wife Myrtle had discovered a
rare avocet or sighted a heron new to the area.[1]

His birdwatching would help to fill the long idle days
ahead, especially in winter when he joined the thousands
of other retired people migrating down the continent toward the warm sun of Florida. Birdwatching promised to be
a gentle sport. He would wander along manicured trails,
looking into the treetops through his binoculars, carefully
tailoring his activities to whatever physical limits the
mounting years might place upon him.

On his way southward he intended to drive through
Washington, D.C., for a meeting of the American Ornithological Union. There he would have the opportunity to talk
with bird people from around the country, particularly a
staff member of the National Audubon Society, Richard H.
Pough, with whom he had corresponded frequently.

All manner of saddening reports about threats to American wildlife filter into the headquarters of the National Audubon Society. Pough, studying the flow of such stories across his desk, was particularly concerned about the bald eagles. The pressure on the big white-headed birds of prey seemed to have mounted steadily. They were losing their remaining nest trees to the advancing land developers and falling victims to irresponsible gunners. The Florida eagles, prior to 1939, were also giving up a large share of their annual egg production to oologists, that band of incurable kleptomaniacs who took thousands of eggs from the nests of wild birds and kept them in carefully labeled storage cases. Oologists even bought bird eggs from country boys employed to locate the nests. A clutch of bald eagle eggs was worth $10, and there seemed to be a steady and growing demand. One estimate placed the number of eggs lost to human nest robbers in those years at one-half the annual production in Florida. Ornithologist Roger T. Peterson tells of one collector proudly displaying a large bucketful of eagle eggs gathered in one season's climbing. At least one Florida collector nailed cleats to the side of nest trees and returned to rob the nests whenever eagles used them.[2]

Whatever the causes, Pough was convinced the eagles were headed for trouble. He also realized that there was much that was not known about the big bird that serves as the United States emblem. Aside from the pioneering work carried out by Dr. Herrick on the Lake Erie shores, the eagle had been largely ignored as a subject for serious study.

Overshadowing all this was one of the more puzzling

unsolved bird mysteries still plaguing the ornithologists. Large parts of the Florida eagle populations vanished from the state during the summer months. Fall, winter, and spring, they would occupy their territories, nesting, raising their young, and lazily circling the Florida sky. But in the hottest months of the year the newly fledged juveniles and the other immature eagles would suddenly depart. No one had ever determined where they went. This missing link in the eagle story might someday be vitally important if the Florida eagles needed help.

Richard Pough gave Broley four eagle bands issued to him on his own banding permit. "Try banding some nestlings," Pough suggested. Broley explained to Pough that as a younger man he could shinny up just about any tree he encountered. Such climbing, however, was not for retired bankers. "Find a boy to do your climbing," Pough suggested, "and if you need more bands I'll send them down to you." With the four eagle bands in his pocket, Broley headed southward toward Tampa.

In the following weeks Broley drove the back roads of west Florida, always watching the tops of the tallest pine trees for the bulky nests of eagles. Meanwhile, he was searching for a boy of proper attitude and agility to climb eagle trees for him. One applicant bragged that he would take a stick and crack the skull of any parent bird that swooped in too close to him. Broley saw he would have to do his own climbing, and he started by designing equipment for the purpose.

At first, he thought the answer might be spikes of the kind used by linemen working for the utility companies, but the wood beneath the pine bark was often hazardously soft.

Next he began building a rope ladder with two long pieces of rope, between which he fitted 12-inch sections of wood as steps.

Then he purchased a supply of 4-ounce lead sinkers. He tied one of these weights to a hundred yards of fishing line and found that he could throw it over the first limb of a pine tree, 40 feet above the ground. This was his first step toward getting the ladder secured in the nest tree. The weight pulled one end of the line back down to him and he tied onto it a section of clothesline which he could then pull up over the limb. Next, he attached a one-inch rope and, using the clothesline, pulled the rope up; finally he used the rope to hoist his new rope ladder up the tree. Once he secured the ladder by tying the bottom of it to the tree trunk, he was ready to start up to the eagles.

Broley early encountered difficulty heaving the lead weight up over the limb. He soon learned why a professional ball pitcher has to work so hard conditioning his arm. Broley's solution was to make a catapult by attaching a large tablespoon to a section of broom handle. The spoon cradled the lead weight with line attached. Then Broley aimed and flipped the weight skyward with the accuracy of a lacrosse player, which he once had been.

Later refinements of this system included a slingshot, which Broley handled with uncanny accuracy, and a fisherman's large casting reel to keep the line from tangling. His 40 pounds of tree-climbing equipment was an ingenious collection of related parts that over the following years helped Broley reach hundreds of eagle nests. From time to time visiting naturalists ascended Broley's rope ladders but seldom with the grace and nimble speed of the retired

banker from Winnipeg. Broley did not go up the face of the
ladder in the usual manner; instead, he climbed the edge
of it with one leg on either side. Once secure on the first
limb, he would use a short rope to help him advance to the
next limb, and from limb to limb he would then work his
way until directly beneath the nest.

At this point he faced his most hazardous challenge.
The nest, shaped either like a giant deep vase with a widely
flared top, or a shallower flat platform, is designed for entry
from the top only, and a birdbander seeking to lift himself
onto it must often swing out into space and pull himself
upward over the edge. Broley designed an iron rod with a
large shepherd's crook on one end and a smaller hook on
the other. From beneath the nest he could sometimes reach
up with this bar and secure the large hook on the nest, place
a foot in the small hook on the other end, and then step out
and swing himself into the nest with the young eagles.

Some nests were too deep for the hook to catch, and
for these Broley carried a shorter rope ladder that he would
swing up and across the nest. Then, after securing it, he
could climb up the side of the nest. Few men had viewed
that southern countryside as Broley now saw it from far
above the palmetto thickets. In the eagle's penthouse, he
could look out over miles of forests, fields, and towns.[3]

There was, however, seldom much time to admire the
view. Broley's challenge was to accomplish his scientific
mission, band the young eagles, and retire to safety at
ground level as quickly as possible. No man is welcomed to
the home of an eagle. The young birds were more of a
threat than the adults. They were usually banded after they
were 5 weeks old; to leave them until they were 11 or 12

weeks old would bring them to the size of their parents. Fully fledged, they might leap from the nest platform as the stranger came aboard.

Once secure in the nest, Broley's first tactic was to grab the bird's left wing and hold it down with one knee while scrambling for the left foot. The young eagle was then helpless because he needed the remaining foot and wing to support himself. Using his pliers, the eagle man would soon attach an official aluminum band to the eagle's left leg.

Broley remembered most vividly the nests to which he climbed when the young birds were nearly ready to fly. For days they had been leaping around their platform, strengthening youthful wing muscles with practice flapping. When, after much clatter and scraping against the tree trunk, a strange invader peers over the edge of the nest, a young bird is likely to launch itself abruptly into the world below.

One such bird, Broley recalled, became entangled in wild grape vines part way to earth and hung there helplessly. Patiently, Broley climbed back down, then worked his way up to the eaglet and disentangled it. As he reached the nest with the wayward youngster, the other eaglet, standing on the edge of the nest, stepped out onto a branch, where it teetered precariously. Very carefully Broley eased the first one back into the nest, but it promptly hobbled out to join the other one. Soon both began to teeter. Then they both fell, but this time their efforts carried them out over water, where they splashed into the lake. Broley again descended the tree. By now the chicks had paddled ashore and were hiding in the palmetto scrub. By the time both were carried back up the tree, the weary Broley had spent 7 hours banding two young eagles.[4]

That first year Broley banded forty-four eagles, more than had ever been banded before in all of Florida. Broley began to get occasional returns from his banded eagles, and from surprisingly distant points. More than a third of the recovered bands were taken from eagles a thousand miles or more up the eastern seaboard from their home nests. One hardy young traveler flew at least 1,600 miles and was finally shot on Canada's Prince Edward Island. Bands recovered from Broley's eagles were sent back to the United States Fish and Wildlife Service from seventeen states and provinces. Richard Pough's idea and Charles Broley's efforts were bringing results. Obviously the immature eagles hatched in Florida were moving northward, some for great distances, spending the last of the hot season, then returning ahead of winter.

Birdbanders have ambivalent feelings about reports of the birds they band. Almost certainly any information on one of his banded eagles would tell of the death of the bird, and for this reason Broley was perhaps happiest when he heard nothing. There were rare stories with happy endings. One day, relaxing in his winter home in Florida, Broley was reading a newspaper sent to him from Ontario when he noted a story about an eagle that had become the best-known bird in Picton, Ontario. The police of Picton had been called to rescue the wounded bird and had then installed it in a large cage in the middle of town. The eagle was wearing one of Broley's bands and he recognized it by number as a bird banded near Picton. According to the report, people in Picton planned to release the eagle on

Timber Island, in Lake Ontario, where other eagles would be expected to care for their wounded. Broley automatically gave the eagle up for dead.

Two years later, he flew to Timber Island with his climbing tools to band young birds in an eagle nest of which he had heard. He rented a boat from an island fisherman, who asked him what he was going to do with all the ropes he carried. Broley told him about his work with eagles, and the fisherman's eyes brightened. Then he retold his favorite eagle story. The police chief of Picton had arrived one day bringing with him a big wounded eagle and asking him to set it free in the forest. But the man put the eagle in the backyard, where it followed him about begging fish and growing steadily stronger. Then, one day, a strange eagle cruised low over the yard. The injured eagle ran down the walk, gained speed, and lifted itself into the air. The last the fisherman saw of it, the bird was off in the distant sky still traveling with the other eagle and still flying strong.[5]

Most of Broley's eagle work was concentrated along the western coast of Florida. There, for 164 miles south from Hernando County, Broley knew of 140 nests in active use by eagles. He found nests at the rate of about one for each mile of coast, a density rivaling that of the best bald eagle habitat of Alaska. Most of these were near salt water, although some were around inland lakes. Broley made notes on the kinds of trees in which these eagles nested. Longleaf pine ranked first, but a few were in towering cypress trees as much as 125 feet above the swamps. When there were no taller trees nearby, Broley even found eagles nesting in black mangroves within 15 feet of the ground.

Broley, accustomed to climbing 100-foot high pines to the
level of the eagles, thought that nesting in mangroves must
be "humiliating" for the "king of the air."

Nests near human dwellings sometimes caused Broley
special troubles. To his delight, he soon discovered that the
majority of Florida people take pride in having the great
birds living nearby. He was arrested three times early in his
banding career by local police rushing to the scene where
neighbors reported a man "robbing the eagle nest." As a
defense measure Broley formed the habit, when going into
a neighborhood searching for nests, of stopping first at the
local police station and explaining his mission. The longer
he worked in Florida, the more widely the "eagle man"
became known, and those who understood the nature of his
task welcomed him warmly.[6]

For 12 years Broley continued his eagle banding. The
Broleys spent their summers in Ontario, where they had a
house on an island in a lake. There, instead of using a
motor, the wiry Broley would row to the mainland to do the
shopping, always keeping himself in top condition for the
strenuous winter of climbing ahead. As the day approached
for his departure to Florida, he put in daily sessions with
the chinning bar. "When I could chin myself eighteen times
without pausing," Broley always said, "I figured I was ready
to climb again." At the age of 70 he still possessed stamina
and strength that younger men envied. He could carry 40
pounds of equipment through the jungle of palmetto on
the hottest days, or wade with it through a cypress swamp
to reach a nest he had heard about. His climbing feats
became legendary. National magazines sent their reporters
and photographers south to go into the field with him. But

few accepted his quiet invitation to climb up to the nests.

Broley's concern for the eagles' future was growing. In the 12 years that he climbed Florida's trees he banded far more than had ever been banded before by all the birdbanders combined throughout the bald eagle's range.[7]

His banding was done mostly in January and February. Florida eagles begin their nesting activities in late September and early October, with repair of the old nest and adding perhaps 2 feet of new sticks to the platform, followed by a mattress of grass or Spanish moss. Some eagles, Broley found, covered their eggs with this material when not incubating and others even piled the Spanish moss up on the windward side of the nest where it served as a windbreak. By April or May, when the summer heat presses down upon Florida, the young eagles are ready for their first cross-country flights. They usually strike out northward and follow the Atlantic coast, cruising, feeding, and learning to survive.

Back in New York, Richard Pough, who had started the ex-banker on this daring enterprise, often worried about the possibilities that Broley might fall from an eagle's nest and crash 90 or 100 feet to the ground.

An old eagle nest adds hundreds of pounds to the branches of the aging tree in which it rests, and the temporary weight of one climbing man nudges the total burden toward that unknown point which is the limit of the tree's strength. Nobody understood the hazards better than Broley. He never climbed a tree that he did not first study thoroughly. Some he did not climb at all.

Only once did he think he might have made a serious mistake. He climbed to a spot just below a giant nest 95 feet above the ground, arranged his ropes, and prepared to go up and into the nest. Everything seemed in order as he clambered over the edge, but in that moment there was an ominous creaking, then a sudden cracking of splitting wood somewhere below him. A large limb supporting one side of the nest broke off and the nest tilted sharply. Broley scurried to a limb that seemed sound, and waited to see if the treetop would hold. The young birds were still inside the nest, apparently secure. Very carefully, Broley worked his way to the ground.

Concerned that the weakened tree might not last out the nesting season, he returned the following day with some two-by-fours. For several hours he climbed up and down the tree, placing braces in position, securing the weakened eyrie. In the following weeks, feeling a sense of guilt for having threatened the eagles' lives, he checked the eyrie frequently. The nest held through the season and the young survived.

Only once did Broley fall in the line of duty. At the end of a successful banding season, he and his wife had driven back to Canada and Broley was standing on a chair storing his climbing equipment in the closet for the summer. The chair tilted, pitching him to the floor. Broley's head hit the edge of a bed, rendering him unconscious.

In Florida eagles fell victim to many hazards. Once there had been twenty active nests around the fishing center of Bradenton on the Florida gulf coast. Ten were destroyed when the nest trees were cut down. Seven more nests were abandoned when land was cleared around them. One was abandoned because a drive-in theater was built too close to it, another because spray planes flew too low over it, and the twentieth because homes were built in the area.

During the early years of his banding, Broley was excited and pleased to find the eagle population so vigorous in Florida: "I found 125 active nests each year—a thrilling experience for any naturalist. By 1946 I was banding some 150 eagles a season."[8]

But in 1947 a saddened Broley found fewer young eagles in the nests: "41 percent of the nests occupied by eagles failed to produce young." The following autumn, Broley drove back to Florida wondering if the situation would be improved. He took along 150 bands. But he found the situation among the big white-headed eagles not better, but worse. Year by year the productivity plummeted, until by 1950 Broley's records revealed that only 22 percent of the occupied nests produced young. That year Broley placed bands on only twenty-one young eagles. He climbed to eighty-two nests in 1951, but only twenty contained eggs that hatched. Again in 1952 only eleven nests contained young eagles, a total of fifteen birds. By 1955 Broley was to report that in all his 100-mile coastal territory he could now find only eight young bald eagles. In slightly more than a decade he had seen the eagle production fall from 103 young to eight. In nest after nest he reported that the adult birds were in residence, but not nesting. Some did not produce eggs, others laid eggs which failed to hatch. Broley had become the first to notice that these birds of prey were really in trouble.[9]

Broley made no pretense of being a scientist. He was a banker turned naturalist, a field worker. Unhampered by the scientist's caution, and unworried about the judgment of his peers, Broley was not afraid to announce what he took to be the cause of the eagles' newly discovered problem. He quickly drew a parallel between the trouble of the eagle and the problems reported by a friend, Cecil Robinson, of Barnsville, Virginia.

Robinson had given his 3-year-old Angus bull phenothiazine at the rate of 2 ounces daily mixed with its feed, as protection against heel flies. After 3 weeks of this medication the bull had become impotent; within a month after the treatment was stopped, the bull regained his potency. The evidence which in 1962 would lead Rachel Carson to publish *Silent Spring* was just beginning to surface.

This story of Robinson's led Broley to recall earlier fish kills by insecticides, and he remembered a report on the possibility that DDT was lowering the productivity of bobwhite quail in Georgia. There was also the fact that a recent large fish kill in Tampa Bay left dead fish whose bodies contained residues of DDT. Broley noted that eagles tend to pick up first those fish most easily taken, the ones that are sluggish or dead. "Is it not possible," he asked, "that a cumulative amount of DDT in eagles has caused sterility?"

Years of tedious laboratory testing would pass, and reams of cautious statements would be issued before there would be a final answer to the direct question which Charles Broley, the eagle man, had asked of the scientific community.

Over Broley's remarkable retirement career he banded more than 1,200 eagles. His eagle work ended with the 1958 season. He had searched as diligently as ever along the same hundred miles of coast where a short time ago he had banded as many as 150 eagles a year. But at the end of the season he had located only one young bald eagle on which to place a band.[10]

Broley died in the spring of 1959, not by falling a hundred feet from the top of a longleaf pine tree, but while fighting a brush fire near his home in Canada.

8

Danger in the Sky

FLYING over the west Texas countryside in his small plane, John Casparis often watched with admiration as eagles rode the updrafts in the rugged canyons of the Davis Mountains. Their maneuvering was accomplished with supreme ease. An eagle soaring swiftly in on the strong winds would sometimes fly directly toward the rocky face of the towering cliffs, and there was no last minute veering off, no turning chicken to avoid a crash. It was as if the eagle could see the wind, therefore knew no fear. At the final moment, although the eagle does nothing to change its course, it is swept effortlessly to the ridgetop as if in an elevator, to soar from sight into the next canyon.

Casparis claimed he learned from the eagles and that the updrafts also helped lift his plane out of the canyons. It might also be said that the eagles should have learned a few things from Casparis. During the 1940s he became a legendary flier in west Texas, and acquired a reputation for his uncanny ability to track eagles through the sky and shoot them. This talent was soon in heavy demand.

The west Texas aerial attack on the eagles began one day when a local rancher drove his pickup truck into Alpine, Texas, and out to the little airport looking for Casparis, who operated a flying service there. While driving across his range that morning the rancher had grown increasingly distraught as, one after the other, he came upon the carcasses of nineteen sheep. The agents of death visited on a flock of sheep may range from pneumonia and scabies through tapeworms and starvation. But to the angry rancher the answer looked far simpler: the animals were dead and soaring overhead was an eagle. What else does one need to know?

Casparis was asked if he had ever given any thought to shooting eagles from his airplane. Casparis, pondering the idea, said he didn't know whether it would work or not because he had never tried it or even heard of anyone trying it. But there was one way to find out. Another day, with the rancher doing the shooting, the two men overtook twelve eagles in the Davis Mountains and dropped them out of the sky with a shotgun. A couple of days later they flew again, and this time they brought to earth nine more eagles.

As Casparis continued his highly efficient bounty hunting system, word began to spread across the state and into eastern New Mexico that this daring flier from over at Alpine had found the real way to kill the cursed eagles. Demands for Casparis's services grew rapidly. Seeking a businesslike system for keeping Casparis and his little fighter plane in the air, local ranchers formed the Big Bend

Eagle Club. The group operated as a cooperative. Each rancher paid dues and could call on the services of the eagle killer when he believed he had a problem, or might be about to suffer losses. Around lambing time there was heavy demand on the pilot's services. Other communities soon began organizing to send gunners aloft in pursuit of the eagles, and "eagle clubs" appeared in Kent, Marathon, Marfa, Fort Stockton, Medina, Del Rio, and San Angelo. "At one time," Casparis told me, "I was flying for four clubs myself here and in New Mexico."[1]

Casparis was an ace said to have few equals among the fliers of west Texas. He flew with the window removed from the plane on his side of the cockpit and performed his executions smoothly and adroitly with a sawed-off shotgun loaded with No. 4 shot. He could come up to a flying eagle from behind, remove his hands from the controls, pick up the gun, lean out the window, shoot, put the gun back, and take the controls before the plane went into any threatening posture. He carried extra weight in the rear of the plane to make the nose rise sharply as he released the controls. Allowed to go too far, the plane would have stalled into a dive. But Casparis needed only moments to shoot an eagle, and he managed alone what other pilots flying against the birds in those years accomplished by carrying a passenger to do their shooting. "When I was younger and my eyes were better," he said, "I wouldn't miss more than one out of twenty. Later I still hit 'em half of the time, and the ones I missed I'd turn around and go back after again."[2]

There is no question that he removed from the western skies large numbers of eagles during his years of flying. In one day in 1948 he killed 28 eagles, his top score for a day's flying. In one year he is said to have killed 1,008, mostly golden eagles. That year, in addition to eagles, he also claimed 315 coyotes, 28 bobcats, and one cougar. His yearly average was listed at 850 eagles and 250 coyotes. I told him I had heard that his lifetime total was 12,000 eagles killed. "That's about right," he said. "I killed about 5,000 coyotes for that matter," he added. Casparis added that there were no longer as many eagles as there once were. "That's because others got in on it too," he said, "in other states." He believes, however, they will come back. "Don't say they don't do damage, because they do, and a man's not going to just stand by while they do it."

As the aerial war on the eagles became part of the accepted pattern of ranch life in west Texas, some noted that this method of eagle killing really had its origin in California before World War II. Early in 1936, a letter from pilot Ben Torrey, of Corning, appeared in the sports section of the San Francisco *Chronicle:* "I use my airplane, which is a three-place biplane. I remove the left door so the gunner can shoot out to the left. I have ribbons taped onto the wires so they will not shoot into the propeller. . . . I recommend a shotgun with about No. 2 shot. At times I am able to fly within 50 feet of the bird by getting behind and slightly over it. We are permitted to kill golden eagles, but not the bald variety. . . . This is something new and I am in the business of taking passenger-hunters out. In an hour's time I usually cover about 70 or 80 miles of territory."

That same year, in the ornithological journal *Condor,* Frederick H. Dale reported competition developing between community eagle shooters through northern California. The Red Bluff *Daily News* reported: "When friends of Floyd Nolta, Willows flier, heard today that Ben Torrey, the Corning aerial wild game hunter, had killed 38 eagles by plane, they said that was pretty good but that Nolta had killed 160." Dale, watching the planes pursue eagles, then inspecting the fallen birds, found at least five that were not golden eagles but bald eagles.[3]

Through the Sacramento valley the golden eagle is a permanent resident. During winter, however, the bald eagles come drifting down from the north for the season and, according to Dale, were "more abundant during that winter season than the Golden Eagle, at least in the country east of Red Bluff." Dale calculated that at least two hundred eagles were shot there that year and that they were predominately bald eagles. Not until four years later was the Bald Eagle Act passed by Congress. One sheep rancher told Dale that he could not see much difference between the destructive tendencies of the two species. "We have lost lambs from our corral," the rancher said. "We feel certain they were taken by eagles. We do not know what eagles killed them, so we kill all the eagles we can." Dale called this "condemnation of the rain because it may bring the flood."[4]

In the next few years, as this brand of "sport" flying spread through western communities, the aerial attack on the eagles intensified. In the frontier ethic, this was an exciting challenge, combining skilled flying and dead-eye aim, all honorably encased in an aura of public service. At last the predatory eagles were meeting their match in the western skies.

As the aerial killing of eagles continued, conservationists were increasingly convinced that the golden eagles could not withstand the drain indefinitely. There was also a growing belief that the protected bald eagles, as well as golden eagles, were being dropped from the skies. Separating the golden eagles from the immature bald eagle is not easy for most observers. And even those pilots capable of making the distinction could not be expected to spare any kind of eagle as they flew out across the lonely range far from any observers. There was no question that bald eagles lived within the Texas range where the eagle clubs were in business. One day, Dr. Walter R. Spofford, professor of ornithology at Cornell University and world renowned as an authority on eagles, observed two immature bald eagles circling over the rugged rocky bluffs of the Muleshoe National Wildlife Refuge in Texas. In the Trans-Pecos of southern New Mexico he found bald eagles "rather common," and in one three-day visit there he spotted nine bald eagles. Dr. Spofford learned of an adult bald eagle trapped near Davis, Texas, but released, and he told of the flier with sixty-three eagles to his credit, who landed one afternoon with a "different kind of eagle." His "different" eagle was a fully mature bald eagle with flashing white head and tail. Although the flier was fined for the offense, the eagle could not be returned to the dwindling population.[5]

As the small planes continued to lift from the airfields and speed through the western skies on the trail of the eagles, conservationists watched with increasing alarm. Man was decimating the eagles, and this conviction prompted the National Audubon Society president, Carl Buckheister, to call his friend Dr. Spofford early in 1963. Buckheister explained to Dr. Spofford that the Audubon

Society was preparing to dispatch a scientist to west Texas, where the eagles were under siege. Did Dr. Spofford have someone in mind who might conduct a study down there, see what kind of eagles were being killed, and perhaps learn if the accused birds were really eating sheep? Dr. Spofford, as he told me one afternoon in his Etna, New York, home, considered only briefly before saying, "I believe I might be interested in handling this one myself." For the next two winters, Dr. Spofford, a slender, tanned, soft-spoken scientist, worked among the Texas ranchers and pilots.

He was astounded to learn that the eagle-conscious sheepmen looked upon Big Bend National Park, that rugged land of arid scrub brush and rocky ledges along the Rio Grande, as a notorious reservoir of breeding eagles, which could spread outward, along with cougar and assorted bobcats, to victimize ranchers over thousands of square miles. The ranchers, conditioned by the government predator control program, had difficulty understanding the apparent dichotomy in which the same government turned around and offered protection to predators within the national park. But Dr. Spofford could see no logic in the "reservoir" idea. "The patent absurdity of this concept," he wrote, "does not seem to have occurred to them."[6] At the time there was not a pair of eagles known to be nesting in the entire Big Bend National Park. At most, according to this eagle authority, the park could have supported ten pairs of eagles. He labeled the national park's contribution to the winter eagle population "insignificant," and added that the same could be said of its production of cougars and bobcats.

Neither, he insisted, could much credence be placed

in the mossy conviction that Mexico was also a grand reservoir of eagles which would, on occasion, flock across the Rio Grande searching for food in the more fertile grazing lands of Texas. Without doubt eagles do cross back and forth over the border as they would cross any other unmarked line within their range. But the eagles of the south, explained Dr. Spofford, "do not migrate." It is when food becomes scarce that the eagles move. Those that historically nest in the south normally have food supplies within their nesting territory the year around. They stay. Eagles concentrating during winter months in the south, he added, were undoubtedly of northern origin, down from the northern states and Canada. Northern eagles have no choice but to move southward as the ground squirrels retire underground for winter, the hoary marmots hibernate, or the fishing waters freeze. Unfortunately for the eagles, their travels bring them to the sheepman's country in the critical season of lambing, when losses are normally high.

Understandably, the eagles concentrate in those lands best suited to raising livestock, because the same grasslands also support large populations of jackrabbits, historic staple food source for the golden eagles. Into the roughest rangelands of west Texas, eastern New Mexico, and northern Mexico the eagles funnel by the hundreds. They are arriving by late autumn, and the sheepmen come to expect a new influx of the hated birds riding the winds with each new storm out of the north.

With the lambing season approaching, the ranchers were quick to alert their eagle shooters so the eagles might be met with a shotgun fusillade. In winter this region attracted a large percentage of all the 8,000 to 10,000 golden eagles believed then to be resident on the North American continent. "It is this population," said Dr. Spofford, "a large part of the total eagle population, which has become not only the concern of the sheep rancher, but also, because of the winter shoot-off, the concern of the nation. The yearly shoot-off," he said, was accounting for "a substantial part of the annual crop of juvenile eagles."[7]

In 1962, at the urging of wildlife scientists and citizen conservationists, the 1940 Bald Eagle Act had been extended to give some federal protection to the endangered golden eagle as well. But the statute was full of loopholes. Pressure from stockmen prompted congressmen to include a provision authorizing the secretary of the interior to grant annual countywide permits for killing golden eagles in western states. These were not to be permits for executing individual birds caught in an act of lamb killing, but broad authority to kill all the eagles possible within a county or state. The first step was for a state governor to send to Washington a letter of request for this special permission. The secretary could then act. Year after year, as a matter of course, sheepmen urged their governors to write for the eagle-killing authorization. It became general practice for the secretary to issue the permits, and the eagle killing continued.

By an amendment to the law, Congress in 1962 finally made it illegal to kill eagles by using either aircraft or poisons. Sheepmen came to the Capitol protesting loudly. They were less concerned about the ban on poisons for eagle killing than they were about bringing the eagle pursuit planes out of the western skies.

Obviously these sheepmen had not changed their thinking about the eating habits of the detested eagles. And, as might be expected, not all of them readily gave up the highly effective method of attacking eagles in the air. Some ignored the laws which said such flying was no longer legal, just as they belittled the repeated studies which made it evident that the eagles were not the culprits they claimed in the loss of lambs. Right into the 1970s a few diehard ranchers continued to carry out their eagle vendetta, hiring aerial gunners, setting traps on cairns and rocky ledges, and always keeping the shotgun ready on the gun rack behind the seat in the pickup.

Helicopters and small fixed-wing aircraft continued to fly against the eagles, sometimes for "sport," sometimes for pay. Some ranchers used their own aircraft, flying across miles and miles of open range where they could see any observer long before he might surprise them in their eagle killing. One seasoned federal game agent explained to me the near impossibility of catching such eagle shooters in the act. "There are many ranchers who don't want the eagles shot," he said, "but those that do can get away with it too easily. Our men have to see them shoot an eagle, then they have to present the evidence, a dead eagle. Even if you are lucky enough to be there and see the eagle shot out of the sky, the chances of finding it are mighty slim. Catching them is more a matter of luck than the result of good planning." The laws that should have protected the eagles were on the books, but eagles continued to fall before the unceasing onslaught.

9

The Chemical Age

WHEN Charles Broley linked the effect with the most obvious cause and made his instant analysis—that DDT was wiping out the eagle population—he spoke from a lonely pulpit. His remarks were largely ignored, especially by members of the agricultural community. Even an able and qualified ecologist making such a suggestion would have met strong resistance, a fact that would be impressed harshly upon biologists in the years ahead.

In the years immediately following World War II the newly available insecticides were being hailed as substances that might at last deliver man from the ravages of the insects. "Prophets of evil tell us," wrote F. C. Bishopp, of the United States Department of Agriculture, "that human overpopulation of the world is approaching, and approaching rapidly; that mass starvation is sure to come . . . if greater production of plant food cannot be stimulated or if new foods cannot be invented." Dr. Bishopp saw an answer in the stopping of waste: "Probably the greatest of these wastes is the tremendous but unnecessary tribute that we pay to insects. In the United States alone, the labor of one million men each year is lost through their damage to crops and to our other vital interests."[1]

To this, Dr. H. L. Haller, also of the United States Department of Agriculture, added: "In a few years it [DDT] has excited the imagination of scientists and laymen alike —and rightly. . . it gives control over those history-old scourges, the body louse, the mosquito, and the fly; and, wonderful to relate, its effect lasts sometimes as long as a year."[2]

Within a few years the DDT story swept the world, and in the United States alone there were more than two thousand articles published on it, "almost all of them," as one jubilant advocate announced, "acclaiming its merits."[3]

Understandably, the prosperous pesticide manufacturers were rushing full speed, not only to meet the demand for DDT, but also to promote and encourage it. The chemical industry composed the message, while professional extension workers in the colleges of agriculture set it to music. Not much thought was given to such occasional words of caution as those of Neil Hotchkiss and Richard H. Pough in the July, 1946, issue of the *Journal of Wildlife Management.* They investigated the experimental spraying of 40 acres in Pennsylvania with 5 pounds per acre of DDT, aimed at gypsy moth control. Before spraying, the population of singing male birds was 3.2 per acre. Three days after spraying there were only "two singing males in the entire area."[4]

Even Dr. Bishopp had seen fit to issue a gentle warning, unusually perceptive in view of the tenor of the times: "Their promiscuous and improper use, however, may lead to other serious problems. There is special danger of destroying the beneficial forms of life, including insect predators, fish, frogs, or even birds by use of a material such as DDT."[5]

The warborne success story of this substance had its beginning in a bleak little laboratory in Germany, where a student completing the requirements of his doctorate at the University of Strasbourg first synthesized the material in 1874 and became the first to describe it. Practical use had to wait for many years of research by later scientists. Finally, during World War II, supplies of the chemical were sent to the United States from Switzerland at a time when thousands of chemicals were being hurriedly tested for all manner of jobs related to the killing of people and other forms of life. In 1939 Swiss scientists had discovered its remarkable properties for killing insects.

Out of this wartime testing effort, DDT was launched to stardom and scheduled for a postwar glamour role. By 1945 men were busily dusting the surfaces of barns, forests, fields, livestock, and people with 33 million pounds of DDT a year.[6] By 1951 the amount had grown to 106 million pounds. Two decades later, the family of pesticides has broadened, and the United States alone is producing 1 billion pounds annually of insecticides, rodenticides, miticides, herbicides, and fungicides. Nor is there any end in sight. It is predicted that the United States will be producing 6 billion pounds of pesticides annually by 1985.[7] This indicates the massive size of the industry aligned against all who would suggest that such substances as DDT might carry threats to the ecosystems into which they are introduced.

As one of DDT's early promoters, a Department of Agriculture worker, expressed it: "Fortunately DDT is a powerful weapon." Two or three ounces sprayed in solution on 1,000 square feet of a dairy barn would free the stable of flies for the whole summer. This, as biologists were to understand later, would become one of the most serious threats arising from the family of chlorinated hydrocarbon pesticides; they were persistent, so much so that the half-life of DDT would eventually be computed at somewhere between 4 and 16 years. Each year, new applications would be added to the fields to reinforce what was already there, and the residues were caught up in the runoff to flow into the waterways or to ride droplets of atmospheric moisture piggyback around the world.

The same year that Broley discovered the disaster descending on his Florida eagles, Joseph A. Hagar made an unnerving observation in Massachusetts. Hagar, deeply interested in birds of prey, was preparing to photograph a pair of nesting peregrine falcons. He had selected an eyrie known to him for years, one that consistently produced fledgling birds. As in previous years, the wild falcons pursued their remarkable aerial courtship and proceeded to nest. There were three eggs and no hint that anything was wrong. But one day Hagar found two of the eggs broken, and the birds soon abandoned the other one. They started over again. This time the nest held four eggs. But three of them failed to hatch. The fourth one hatched, but the chick died in the nest. For three more years the pair continued to return to their eyrie, but clutch after clutch of their eggs failed to hatch, until they finally vanished and did not come back.[8]

Meanwhile there were early reports of mass kills of robins and other songbirds in cities and on university campuses where trees were being heavily dosed with DDT compounds for the control of Dutch elm disease.

Then farmers began to notice disturbing changes out in the dairy barns where DDT had become the standard weapon against flies. The wonder insecticide seemed to be losing its potency as a fly killer. Flies, through selective survival, were developing DDT-resistant strains.[9]

This rapidly acquired resistance revealed a frightening ability of some insects to overcome the chemical which had promised to deliver mankind from such pests. In California the Mosquito Abatement Districts, with a great sigh of relief, had begun spraying DDT against mosquitos in 1947. But within two years the mosquitos developed significant resistance to DDT. Then some districts quickly switched weapons and began using toxaphene, and by 1951 mosquitoes there were showing resistance to this chemical also. Next came parathion, with similar results; then methyl parathion. One after the other, the mosquitoes adapted to meet each new chemical weapon sprayed upon them, proving perhaps that man through chemistry can play a leading role in creating bigger and stronger bugs—thus fostering the need for increasingly potent insecticides.[10]

One species of particular interest is *Culex tarsalis*, the carrier of equine sleeping sickness that has killed as many as fifty horses in California in a single year, and as many as twelve hundred during epidemics in Texas. Indiscriminate spreading of pesticides is believed to account for this insect's prominence. Today more than two hundred insect pests are known to be resistant to one or more chemical insecticides.

As biologists studied DDT and related organochlorines, they became increasingly convinced that man had created a monster. From barnyards, fields, lawns, and forests, DDT residues washed down to streams, lakes, and estuaries to work into the natural food chains. The trail of the chemical led upward, from prey to predator, to the very top of the food pyramids. In this manner the concentrated residues found their way to the eagle nest.

Slowly and methodically biologist Rachel Carson brought together the abundant evidence against DDT presented in *Silent Spring*. Miss Carson and her supporters had challenged a powerful group. The chemical industries, along with their associates within the United States Department of Agriculture and the land grant colleges, lined up against all who suggested that more chlorinated hydrocarbons were being used than the environment could safely tolerate. Wherever voices of warning were raised, the multi-million-dollar chemical industry rushed to silence them. It is true that much of the evidence presented against DDT seemed circumstantial. The fact that birds died following the spraying of an orchard only left the manufacturers repeating their litany, "There is no evidence that DDT is the cause of death."

While these discussions dragged on over the years, eagles, ospreys, peregrines, pelicans, and others slid steadily closer to extinction. Obviously, if anything was to be done in behalf of the creatures endangered by the chlorinated hydrocarbons, there would have to be some "proof" that the chemicals did kill wildlife, in particular the birds of prey at the tops of their food pyramids. It was not enough to analyze the dead bodies of eagles sent to Patuxent Wildlife Research Center in Maryland and find that they did indeed contain residues of DDT or its metabolites. Such claims would be met with the rebuttal that establishing the presence of the chemicals did not prove them the cause of death.

Therefore in 1961 a test using bald eagles was set up at an experimental fur farm at Petersburg, Alaska, one of the few places where eagles still seemed to prosper. During the early winter, when eagles concentrated along the Chilkat River near Haines to feed on chum salmon, twenty-seven of the birds were captured in weakened steel traps set on stumps where the eagles normally perched. The plan, once the captive eagles were installed in their new pens, was a simple one. The aim was to find what level of DDT in the tissues would bring death to a bald eagle. Some of the birds fed high levels of DDT died, thus proving to most that DDT *can* kill a bird. The lethal level for bald eagles was established at about 160 parts per million in their food.[11] This, however, is a level of contamination to which a wild bird would perhaps never be exposed. There was, however, the more puzzling problem of how sublethal levels of such chemicals in the tissues of adult birds might lead to failure of their eggs to hatch or their young to survive.

Meanwhile, in England, Derek A. Ratcliffe knew that the troubles being experienced by eagles and peregrines in America were likewise plaguing the birds of Great Britain. He had available for study the records of 109 peregrine falcon nests visited by British falconers between 1904 and

1950, and in only 3 nests during nearly half a century had the falconers discovered broken eggs. Ratcliffe compared this with nests visited between 1960 and 1966. In that brief period, when 68 nests were known, 47 had been found with broken eggs.[12]

He was impressed with the thinness of the shells. This led him to begin inspecting other recent peregrine egg shells to see if they also seemed unduly thin. One after the other, the shells collected in recent years seemed to him thin, light in weight, and delicately fragile. He needed older shells against which he might compare these recent ones, and this led him into the museums, to collections of eggs from before the rise of DDT. He found that these pre-DDT eggs averaged 3.81 grams, as compared to 3.09 grams for those taken in 1946 and 1947. The difference in weight amounted to a striking 18.8 percent between peregrine egg shells before and after introduction of DDT.[13]

This set off a flurry of weighing and measuring egg-shell thickness in the United States, first at the University of Wisconsin and later in other centers of research. With agonizing slowness other investigations followed over the years. At Patuxent Wildlife Research Center, a flock of mallard ducks fed a diet containing 10 parts per million DDT suffered a 75 percent decrease in hatching success.[14] In another test the Patuxent staff set out to observe the effects of DDT on the breeding success of a bird of prey under controlled conditions. What was needed, they reasoned, was a population of captive birds of prey whose living conditions could be controlled and whose food consumption could be manipulated and measured. One such bird that had occasionally been bred in captivity was the smallest American member of the true falcon family, the beautifully marked little sparrow hawks often seen hovering over open fields from which they take mice and insects.

Large, roomy flight pens with screened tops and sides were constructed in a quiet corner of the sprawling research complex, and thirty-six identical flight cages partitioned off. Into each flight cage went a healthy pair of sparrow hawks. Plans called for dividing the colony of sparrow hawks into three groups of twelve cages each, and giving each one a special ration. One group, the control, received food free of any insecticides, the second group ate rations into which the investigators mixed DDT and dieldrin at about the rate sparrow hawks would encounter them in the wild, while the third group received food with a high level of DDT and dieldrin.

All three groups produced about the same number of eggs. But it soon became evident that there were dramatic differences in the success these test birds were to have with their nesting efforts. Those that were on a clean diet hatched 84 percent of their eggs, those on DDT and dieldrin levels similar to what they might encounter in nature hatched only 64 percent, and the birds fed higher levels hatched only 59 percent. For the birds consuming insecticides, the drop in reproductive success ranged from 27 to 62 percent. In addition, the eggs of all groups were carefully checked in the laboratory; those birds given pesticides produced eggs with shells ranging from 8 to 17 percent thinner than those produced in the control group.[15]

Here was evidence that should have impressed even the chemical manufacturers. Their technique, however, was either to ignore such findings or to laboriously pick apart the methodology of the experiments, thereby attempting to cast doubt on their validity. Seeing their lucrative poison-manufacturing enterprise threatened after two decades of almost complete freedom, the chemical companies continued to react angrily to mounting evidence and to delay through seemingly endless court action every effort to limit the spreading of DDT.[16]

Scientists still searched for the exact sequence of physiological steps within the bird's body that would reveal how DDT or DDE disturb the reproductive processes. The presence of organochlorines, as chemist Dr. David Peakall had shown at Cornell, appears to stimulate production of a liver enzyme which, in turn, destroys estrogen, the female hormone responsible for controlling much of the reproductive process, including production of calcium and the highly critical timing of its transference for eggshell formation in the oviduct.

Eggshells are formed in three layers, and the middle layer ordinarily gives the egg its greatest strength. This, as two scientists at the University of California at Davis demonstrated in 1971, is also the layer most severely damaged by the bird's consumption of organochlorine pesticides. Dr. L. Z. McFarland and R. L. Garrett fed a test group of Japanese quail a diet containing pesticides at levels similar to what the birds might have obtained in the wild. They then used a scanning electron microscope to study the shells of the eggs produced, comparing them with eggshells from birds fed clean rations. Cross-sections of shell were magnified until they resembled sponge cake. The surface of the shells from birds consuming as little as 5 parts per million of pesticides over a 3-week period were pitted with deep crevices and weakened by networks of tiny microscopic cracks. The net of evidence against the devastating damage of organochlorines was tightening.[17]

Even though the thin-shelled eggs may not break, embryos may die or newly hatched chicks may not survive. Quite low levels of DDE, 2.8 ppm, will cause as much as 10 percent loss of eggshell weight.[18] Then the rate of thinning slows and larger amounts are needed to further affect the weight of the shell. This varies with species. Some investigators have suggested that parent birds carrying high levels of chlorinated hydrocarbons suffer nervous stress, rendering them less capable as parents and more inclined to move around in the nests, thereby bringing increasing hazards to the eggs.

The list of birds suffering the effects of pesticide poisoning has reached well beyond the eagles and other birds of prey to include more than forty species, most of them at or near the tops of their food pyramids.[19] Eggs of bald eagles and brown pelicans have been found in the nests formed with no shells at all.

During the quarter of a century over which these facts were ferreted out and compiled, the wave of death continued. In those years the breeding peregrine falcons vanished from all of eastern America until, by 1970, only in the northern and western fringes of their original North American range could they be found nesting. Meanwhile the bald eagles dwindled in numbers throughout most of their range and the southern race joined the world's list of rare and endangered species, undoubtedly in large degree as a result of the free-wheeling use of chlorinated hydrocarbon pesticides following World War II.

Unfortunately, these pesticides are among the world's

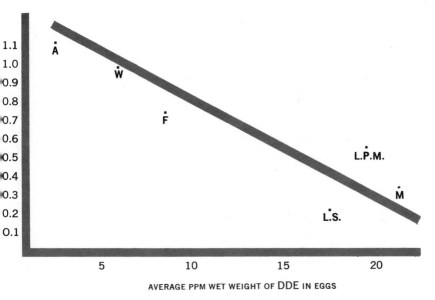

AVERAGE PPM WET WEIGHT OF DDE IN EGGS

Relationship between productivity of six bald-eagle populations and DDE content of their eggs (courtesy National Audubon Society)

A = Alaska	**L.P.M.** = Lower Peninsula Michigan
W = Wisconsin	**L.S.** = Lake Superior shoreline
F = Florida	**M** = Maine

most widely traveled man-made chemicals. By air and water, and through living food chains, they have floated, drifted, and migrated to every corner of the earth. Petrels living on oceanic islands far from any apparent source of DDT are endangered because of their thin-shelled eggs. Polar bears in the Arctic and seals in the Antarctic carry DDE in their tissues.[20] People throughout the world carry chlorinated hydrocarbons in their tissues. For eagle, man or moose there seems no total escape from the chemical pollution of the environment. Americans carry DDE in their fatty tissues at a rate of about 8 parts per million, which is higher than the Food and Drug Administration allows in meats sold for human consumption.[21] The significance of such chlorinated hydrocarbons to the health of the human body over a long period of years is a subject about which medical science still knows very little. Investigators working with rats, however, have discovered that DDT is capable of causing cancerous tumors and, in heavy dosage, genetic mutations as well.[22]

In the 5 years following 1961, every eagle on which technicians performed post mortems at the federal government's Patuxent Wildlife Research Center carried residues of one or more chlorinated hydrocarbon pesticides.[23] Inevitably, when a population of eagles carries a level of chlorinated hydrocarbon pesticides as high as 20 parts per million, that population is declining and disappearing. This has been the situation in Maine, where unhatched eggs were found to carry 23 parts per million. As C. Eugene Knoder, the National Audubon Society's associate director of research, pointed out in 1970, "The highest concentrations of pesticides occur in states with the poorest production of eagles."[24] To this, Frank Ligas, Audubon biologist, adds, "It is more than coincidence that two of Maine's most polluted rivers, the Kennebec and Androscoggin, flow into Merrymeeting Bay, and the eagles in that area lay eggs every year but have not hatched a single one since 1963."[25] By 1970, investigators considered the Maine eagle population doomed. Sadly, this is also true around the Great Lakes, once a region where eagles built their nests all along the timbered shores. The few shells available for checking in 1969 were found to carry 56 parts per million DDE, in addition to significant levels of heptachlor epoxide, dieldrin, and PCBs. Sergej Postupalsky, of the University of

Wisconsin, announced in 1971 that "Lake Superior eggshells are 21 percent thinner and 24 percent lighter than pre-pesticide shells."[26]

In spite of the evidence against DDT and other poisons, the Department of Agriculture, siding with the chemical industry, steadfastly resisted all pleas to limit the application of these wide-spectrum, long-lasting killers. Production went onward and upward. What could not be sold in the United States was shipped around the world. About 70 percent of the DDT produced in the United States is shipped to other countries. This amounts to mass poisoning of the world's biosphere, as winds, waters, and biological food chains are no respecters of political boundaries. It is possible that sophisticated control methods aimed at individual pests and specific uses will be designed as mankind enters a new age of environmental awareness. From all appearances, however, the crude pest control methodology of the recent past has already certified extinction for many of the wild creatures with which man shares the earth.

The fact remains that the burgeoning human population faces food shortages that promise to become increasingly severe—and that pest control does increase the harvest. The challenge is to reap the large harvest without so polluting the environment that nontarget organisms, man included, are brought to the threshold of sickness or early death.

As the true nature of persistent wide-spectrum insecticides has become increasingly evident, there has been growing interest in such biological controls as predatory insects, sex attractants, gene mutation techniques, and diseases specific to the target pests. This approach will not, as is sometimes envisioned by its advocates, replace chemicals so much as it will be used in conjunction with them. Solving specific problems by one or more agents, biological or chemical, while eliminating the widespread use of persistent "hard" pesticides, is the direction in which pest control is, hopefully, headed. This may, of course, be academic; the family of eagles may already be doomed by the DDT we have sprinkled so freely over the earth.[27]

The government has moved, although sluggishly, toward eliminating the use of DDT in agriculture and forestry. But DDT is only one of a whole family of chlorinated hydrocarbon poisons available. After a quarter of century of DDT, the debate continues—not only about DDT but about the other long-lasting, nonselective chemical poisons. "It is foolish and stupid in my opinion," says Dr. Clarence Cottam, director of the Welder Wildlife Foundation in Texas and former career administrator in the Bureau of Sport Fisheries and Wildlife, "to outlaw the use of DDT, which I favor being outlawed, and at the same time permit the more dangerous and more potent chlorinated hydrocarbons to be used with little or no restraint." Specifically, he included dieldrin, heptachlor, aldrin, and mirex.[28]

The bald eagle has faced many enemies. But this massive chemical attack has proved the most devastating of all. Shooting, nest-robbing, electrocution, and even habitat destruction all become more serious as a result of the pesticide deaths. As the number of eagles becomes smaller and smaller, every single individual removed from the remaining population constitutes a tragedy, another major step along the path toward extinction.

10

A Search for Eagles

AMONG the scattered observers attempting to keep close watch on the affairs of the bald eagles during the 1950s there was a growing sense of conviction that the national bird was speeding toward its hour of greatest crisis. In East Moline, Illinois, Elton Fawks, taking part annually in the Christmas bird counts of the Tri-City Bird Club, noticed that the proportion of young in the wintering populations of bald eagles was falling. During the winter of 1958–59, 18 percent of the eagles he recorded were immature, but a year later the percentage had dropped to 15 percent, and the next year to 13 percent.[1]

Elsewhere in the country other ornithologists recorded changes. Maurice Broun, curator of the famed Hawk Mountain Sanctuary in southeastern Pennsylvania, had kept records of his observations of the passing hawks and eagles since 1931. This is a magnificent place for hawk watchers, a mountain ridge where winds out of the west meet the mountains and are deflected skyward. These rising currents are known to the birds migrating out of the north: they set their wings and come down the ridges. Then, where the ridges are close together at Hawk Mountain, the traveling birds concentrate in narrow skyways, to the delight of observers on the ground with binoculars.

In particular Broun watched the returning bald eagles. Until 1945 those he saw passing through the sanctuary were 36.5 percent immature. Then the composition began to change, with the percentages of young eagles becoming lower. In the years between 1954 and 1960 only 23.1 percent were immature.[2]

Beginning about 1962, Jackson M. Abbott, a noted eagle observer of Alexandria, Virginia, also began recording lower percentages of immature eagles in the Chesapeake Bay area, where the birds have long nested and have also concentrated for winter. And no one concerned about the eagles could forget Charles Broley's discovery that the hatching success of bald eagle eggs had dropped from 75 percent to 33 percent in Florida.

A gradual attrition, had it been detected, might not have been surprising. Since the earliest settlers sloshed ashore on the continent the bald eagles had been giving ground to habitat destruction and suffering from shooting. By 1859 the Cleveland Academy of Natural Sciences had reported: "The eagle was of more frequent occurrence during the early settlement of Ohio, than at the present day."[3] By 1903 nesting eagles had already been driven from the shores of southern Wisconsin lakes by the invasion of summer resorts.[4] And in 1940, prior to the recent precipitous plunge of the eagle, Ira N. Gabrielson and

Stanley G. Jewett wrote of the northern bald eagle: "Examining our own notes, we find that it has become rather an uncommon bird in Oregon, except along the coast where a number of pairs still breed."[5]

After World War II the downfall of the bald eagle suddenly began to gain astounding momentum. The Audubon Society has since reported figures that show breeding bald eagle declines ranging from 50 to 60 percent in various sections of the country, along with nesting failures ranging from 55 to 96 percent. And basic questions about the eagles still could not be answered. The bald eagle had been the country's national symbol for almost two centuries, but only sketchy information had been marshaled about how the eagle fared in the changing natural world. The most knowledgeable ornithologists, the best-traveled students of the birds of prey, could do no more than guess at how many bald eagles still lived on the continent. Reliable details on their seasonal movements were minimal, while exact figures on their nesting success were not known. It was known only that the bald eagle was in serious trouble; the reason for it, although suspected, remained to be proved.

The problem was discussed with increasing frequency in the aging red brick building then serving as headquarters for the National Audubon Society in New York City. John Baker, the society's president, eventually called in staff biologist Richard L. Cunningham, told him of his growing fears for the eagle, and asked him to begin concentrating on the problems of the national bird. Cunningham could give the eagle only part of his research time, but this, over the following 2 years, was sufficient to convince Baker and others that the hour had come to mount a crash program to see what was really happening to the American bald eagle.[6]

Down in the Florida Keys the Audubon Society had a skeleton research staff, consisting primarily of Alexander Sprunt IV, a tall, sandy-haired, professional wildlife biologist, and it was to "Sandy" Sprunt that Baker now turned. What was needed was a continentwide study of the bald eagle, and in 1960 Sprunt became the leader of a new Continental Bald Eagle Research Project, with three immediate objectives and a 5-year timetable. Along with other knowledgeable wildlife research people around the country, he wanted to find out how many bald eagles were left, where they were, both in the nesting season and in winter, and particularly how they were faring in producing young to replace themselves.

As he began outlining the first full-scale population survey ever made of the national bird, Sprunt quickly learned that hundreds of people throughout the eagle's broad range were eager to help. In reply to his call for help a flurry of field notes, as well as suggestions for marshaling the country's biologists and bird watchers, began arriving on his desk. Fieldmen with the National Forest Service, the Bureau of Sport Fisheries and Wildlife, and the National Park Service all joined the effort.[7]

Elton Fawks, of East Moline, Illinois, had visited with Charles and Myrtle Broley in 1954, and together they had decided that the spotty information on the distribution and status of the bald eagle should be brought together. Fawks wrote a letter which became widely distributed throughout the United States, was quoted in *Audubon,* and picked up by

news services. Reports on eagles had since been sifting into
Fawks's home. This project was considerably greater than
one man could hope to handle, and Fawks happily blended
his census work into the Audubon project.

The mystery of the wintering populations was of special interest, and Sprunt pored over recent studies of wintering eagles both in Iowa and Illinois, and consulted with
their authors. In fall and early winter eagles were apparently funneling from widely scattered northern breeding
territories, coming down the Mississippi valley to concentrate around open waters where they could find fish and
other food. This led Sprunt to consider the possibility of a
"winter inventory of eagles which might be developed into
an annual count providing an index to the population."

He wrote first to managers of national wildlife refuges,
who provided him with a rich store of figures on wintering
populations. Federal field workers became willing and
valued contributors to the eagle search. Next, the Audubon
research chief designed a questionnaire for all who might
want to help count the eagles. There were more copies of
the new questionnaire reproduced than there were eagles
to be found south of the Canadian border. Four thousand
questionnaires went out to government workers, university
ornithology departments, falconers, local Audubon clubs,
lockmasters on the Mississippi and its tributaries, and everyone else who might be at all interested. The response, in
Sprunt's enthusiastic words, "was immediate and overwhelming." Some observers sent in records of eagle sightings they had been keeping for many years. Others began
reporting to Sprunt every time an eagle flew into view.
Among the eagle reporters watching the skies and scanning

the lakeshores and riverbanks that winter were a housewife in the Aleutian Islands, a forester in Newfoundland, and a towboat captain on the Mississippi. Wildlife employees in many states, particularly Ohio, Missouri, Kentucky, and Pennsylvania, spent long hours in the field searching for the eagles. Hundreds of individuals had joined in the effort to count the wintering eagles.

For three winters these January counts went on, and each time the census revealed a total of about 3,700 bald eagles in the United States, exclusive of Alaska. This population is more than twice the number of bald eagles within the United States during the summer months, when many of the eagles have returned to their northern nest sites across Canada. The census revealed that eagles were still found sometime during the year in all states except Hawaii. But each year the nationwide percentages of immature bald eagles continued to fall, going from 26.5 percent in 1961, to 23.7 the following year, and 21.6 percent in 1963.[8]

This growing storehouse of figures began to reveal where the eagles spend their winters, and also the patterns of the annual movements. Instead of being spread evenly across the country, the bald eagles concentrate in four major geographic areas, which could now be marked on the map. Nearly half of all the eagles counted in January were found in the Middle West, around open waters along the Mississippi valley from southern Minnesota southward to northwestern Tennessee. This is apparently a recent development, following construction of the navigation dams around which there are frequently open water and concentrations of fish.

Another concentration was found in the Northwest,

where the bald eagles wintered along the coast, the major rivers, and in the national wildlife refuges of Washington, Oregon, Idaho, and Montana. In this corner of the country eagle census takers located 742 eagles, 20 percent of the total.

Third in the list of regions was Florida, which during January of 1962 had at least 14 percent of the country's wintering eagles south of Alaska.

Still another concentration was delineated along the coast of the Middle Atlantic states, where 6 percent of the country's bald eagles were found wintering, primarily in Virginia and Maryland.

About 13 percent of the total bald eagle population was not to be found in any of these major areas, but was widely scattered in singles, pairs, and little groups throughout twenty-four states.[9]

As they studied the accumulating records, the eagle authorities began to realize that wintering eagles away from their nesting territories move about restlessly, from one feeding and roosting area to another. As eagles leave an area, new recruits come in from elsewhere and replace them. Throughout the winter this random shifting of populations continues, except for about a month in January, when the populations seem to stabilize. By February the movement has started again, this time northward, back toward the nesting territories, and this slow northward shifting continues into April, with the unmated immature birds returning last. But there is a variety in the habits of eagles. Adult eagles that can find food the year around, as they can in Florida and parts of Alaska, usually spend the entire year in or near their nesting territory.

Now that the Continental Bald Eagle Project had yielded its facts on total populations and their winter distribution, Sprunt was ready to move on to the next part of his assignment. What was greatly needed was a closer look at the biology of the bald eagles. The Fraternal Order of Eagles and the World Wildlife Fund contributed funds for the project, and again, as a beginning, a questionnaire was drawn up and distributed to all who would be helping to study the nesting eagles. Where were the nests? What kind of trees were used by the eagles? How successful were the birds in raising young? These and numerous other questions promised the most comprehensive look yet at the status of the country's remaining bald eagles.[10]

In the Chippewa National Forest in northern Minnesota, biologist John Mathisen began using the new form to record his data on the active nests he had under study. So did Sergej Postupalsky, working on the nesting eagles of Michigan, and field observers elsewhere. Characteristically, these research field men are driven by a compulsive interest in eagles so intense that no weather discourages them, no tree looks too tall to scale, and no amount of wilderness hiking or boating seems too much to ask. When Postupalsky goes into the forest of Michigan searching out eagle nests, he travels with Jack Holt, who does his climbing. I first met Jack one spring day several years ago when he knocked at my front door to ask if I wanted to accompany him into the nearby woods where he intended to band the young of a pair of great horned owls that had serenaded us in the middle of night during the previous winter. But the owl nests are seldom as challenging as the ascent to the home of the bald eagle. Jack recalled vividly a certain white pine in northern Michigan, towering above the earth and holding a massive eagle nest in its crown. He talked about the day in May when he first climbed this pine. "That may be the highest eyrie in Michigan," he said. "The first branch of the giant pine, with its diameter of nearly 10 feet, was a full 70 feet above the ground, and the nest was at least 40 feet above that. That nest was so far above me it was an awesome sight." The climb was long and slow, partly because of what Jack insisted was "petrifying fear." He swung out to the edge of the broad nest, "Tarzan style," and climbed aboard.

As Jack finished banding the first eaglet he glanced upward. "There, coming in a gentle stoop toward the eyrie, was the unmistakable form of the old male with a red squirrel in tow." The adult eagle was winging in, unaware that anything unusual was under way; then, at last, it saw Jack in the nest with its young. "He was so shocked," Jack reported, "that he dropped the squirrel." But the old eagle had instant second thoughts, and folding his enormous wings plummeted after the tumbling squirrel. There was a moment during which both squirrel and eagle seemed to Jack to be coming directly toward him, and there was little he could do about it "except shut my eyes and brace for the impact."

He heard the squirrel tumble through the foliage below him, then a powerful rush of air through primaries as the eagle checked his speed with those long, broad wings and fanned tail, and pulled out of his dive close beside Jack crouching in the nest. The eagle then spiraled upward on pounding wings, uttering loud, shrill cries of protest but leaving Jack in uneasy possession.

Nesting surveys for the researchers involved a constant search for new pairs of eagles, then at least two visits to the area occupied by each pair of birds to see how they were progressing at raising young. In areas where there were several nests to check, the initial survey was often done from an aircraft, sometimes enabling the observer to look down into the nest and count the eggs. Then later, when the eggs had hatched and the young should be well along, there was a second visit. This too was completed by air unless the young were to be banded. In this way records were made of the eggs produced and of the eagles' success in raising their young. The United States Bureau of Sport Fisheries and Wildlife, the National Forest Service, the National Park Service, and the Bureau of Land Management had contributed their biologists' observations. The information was pooled, and as they had with the wintering populations, the eagle researchers could now at last map the nesting areas of the bald eagle. If Alaska and Canada were excepted, there were no more than perhaps 700 mated pairs of bald eagles still attempting to produce young.

There are a few bright spots in the story of the eagle. Perhaps the most encouraging news comes from south Florida, where Dr. William B. Robertson, Jr., senior scientist at Everglades National Park, has been studying eagles since he first began flying over that sprawling wetland in 1958. Of some 200 pairs of breeding eagles known to live in Florida, about 60 live south of the Tamiami Trail, nearly all of them around the estuaries lying within lands under federal protection, the National Park, and the national wildlife refuges within the lower Florida Keys. Dr. Robertson, after watching the 50 to 55 breeding pairs occupying territories inside the National Park, finds happily, that this population of bald eagles is "essentially in its primitive condition. I know of no evidence," he explained, "that the region ever supported a larger number of nesting bald eagles. The population is stable and is reproducing at a rate more than adequate to maintain its numbers."[11]

These adults are resident birds. Once they acquire mates and territories they are established for life and apparently do not leave the refuge of their south Florida home even seasonally. The first year young, as Broley's early work somewhat to the north indicated, may migrate along the east coast. Whether this is definitely true for the young eagles hatched south of the Tamiami Trail, however, is not yet known.

According to the surveys, there were another 110 pairs in Minnesota, 80 pairs in the wilder parts of Wisconsin, and about that many more in Michigan. These, plus the 200 Florida pairs, accounted for considerably more than half of the country's southern bald eagles. Of the rest, about 20 pairs were in Yellowstone and the Tetons, and about another dozen pairs were in Montana and Idaho. Perhaps another 10 pairs nested along the Mississippi River, 5 or 6 around Reelfoot Lake, 1 pair in Missouri, and 2 at Horseshoe Lake in Illinois.

In 1971, southwest Ontario had only five known nests. All around the shores of the Great Lakes the bald eagles were down to fewer than two dozen pairs, with almost no reproduction in eagle nests near the shores of the Great Lakes.

From Louisiana, meanwhile, came reports of only 4 or

5 pairs, while Texas still had a total of 5 pairs living along its gulf coast. In Maine, where eagle populations had been plunging downward, there were now about 35 to 40 known pairs remaining. None remained along the east coast from Maine southward to Chesapeake Bay. Around Chesapeake Bay, a region known within the memory of many for its large and prospering eagle population, there were only about 60 pairs. Along the coast of North and South Carolina, eagles were still found in dwindling numbers totaling perhaps no more than 25 pairs. None were any longer known to live in Georgia.

In this manner the countdown on the nesting bald eagles continued. No one could be certain how the eagles of Canada fared, but the eagle students knew now that many of the eagles nesting in Canada came south to swell the numbers of wintering birds along the Mississippi and elsewhere. They searched the winter census figures for clues, and their best estimates placed the breeding population of Canada's bald eagles at between two and four thousand. Alaska, the one big bright spot in the bald eagle picture, still listed about 4,000 pairs. This brought the world's total number of bald eagles to perhaps no more than 8,000 breeding pairs, most of them in Alaska and Canada.

These coordinated observations were also to bear out the earlier findings of Charles Broley. As Alexander Sprunt reported after his 1962 survey, the bald eagle is not producing as many young as it should. Of the 368 nests studied across the country that year, only 44 percent succeeded in producing young, a total of 224 fledglings. Nearly half of the successful nests were in one state—Florida.[12]

At last, through a monumental, nationwide, coordinated effort, the jigsaw pieces had been assembled and the concerned students of the bald eagle could see the picture. The conclusion was neither pretty nor encouraging.

The Continental Bald Eagle Project had served its purpose. Sprunt's assignment was ending. But his interest in the fate of the national bird was as strong as ever. As he visited and corresponded with others across the country who had played their roles in the survey, he knew their work would not stop completely. Individual ornithologists who have followed the eagle trails through the forests and along the waterways will go on observing the giant birds, studying their occasional rare successes, and watching their failures, still hopeful that they are not observing the last days of the king of America's native birds.

11

Intolerance
and Poison

AUTUMN brings eagles migrating down out of the
Canadian Rockies to stay the winter in Wyoming. They soar
along the ridges of the Bighorn Mountains and in from the
Powder River country until their routes converge around
Immigrant Gap, 9 miles west of Casper. There, a dozen
miles southwest of the city, the eagles concentrate in winter
along the valley of the north Platte River.

Here the wild winds from the northwest, after crossing
the rolling plains, encounter a great sandstone cliff rising
to heights of 300 feet or more. The rock wall turns the
winds upward, and the eagles rise on these updrafts, soaring effortlessly in the blue western sky, gaining a magnificent view of all creatures, large and small, that move upon
the broad landscape below. As long as the winds hold and

the eagles live, this aerial show promises unforgettable memories to all who are privileged to see it. But the eagles coming to winter in this lonely place in the heart of Wyoming have been handed a bitter lesson.

Nearby is Jackson Canyon, 3 miles long, narrow, twisting, rock-walled, its rim fringed with the dark greens of towering ponderosa pines. Jackson Canyon, with its lacework of dead pines for perching, has given the eagles a secure refuge for roosting and resting. When not soaring on the updrafts along the Platte, they could be seen there perched in the trees by anyone visiting Jackson Canyon in winter. When hunting, the eagles fan out over the surrounding rangelands, perhaps for 25 miles or more.[1]

Eagles are not alone in their claim on the wild and lonely Jackson Canyon. This is an adventureland often explored by schoolboys with time to spare, and on Saturday, May 1, 1971, two high school seniors, Gordon Krause and Bruce Wampler, left Casper to hike and rock-climb in the Canyon. They walked about a mile into Jackson Canyon, where they suddenly came upon the remains of two bald eagles. Nearby they found more, for a total of seven birds. They hurried off in search of the ranch owner, reported what they had found, and returned to town, where they also told the game protector as well as members of the Murie Audubon Society.

The local Audubon members called Robert K. Turner, Rocky Mountain regional representative of the National Audubon Society. Early the following day a little group of Audubon Society members left Casper for Jackson Canyon, taking Bruce Wampler and Gordon Krause along as guides. They searched the canyon, and when the saddened hikers returned to their cars they carried the remains of thirteen dead eagles.

Turner promptly placed a call for his boss, Charles H. Callison, executive vice president of the National Audubon Society, and found him in Washington, where he was prepared to testify the next morning before a congressional committee.

Early Monday morning Callison called the office of Nathaniel Reed, newly appointed assistant secretary of the interior. "I alerted him," Callison later reported in *Audubon* magazine, "that at 8:00 P.M., when representatives of several organizations were scheduled to meet with him in his office, I would make an oral but formal request to the department for immediate and exhaustive investigation of the illegal slaughter in Wyoming." Without question the high level of public interest in the bald eagle's plight would make the Wyoming eagle tragedy nationwide news.[2]

By the time the conservationists assembled in Reed's office that afternoon, and Callison registered his statement, the assistant secretary already had his people at work on the case. He had quickly summoned Charles H. Lawrence, long-time chief of the Division of Management and Enforcement, and within twenty-four hours Lawrence, accompanied by a team of investigators, was enroute to Wyoming. Along with state wildlife officers, the federal agents spread over the surrounding countryside continuing the search for dead eagles. Few people believe they found all the poisoned eagles that must have fallen on the broad, sparsely occupied lands of Wyoming that winter, but the total mounted to forty-eight, including both golden and bald eagles, and was enough to shock citizens across the nation.

Reaction to this eagle disaster was instant. Western papers led off with strong editorials and accounts of the crimes as detailed as if the victims of the massacre had been humans. Wire services carried the stories. Network television crews traveled to Wyoming to report on the deaths, and national magazines covered the gruesome event.

Almost immediately, the rising tempo of public reaction was felt in the offices of congressmen in Washington. Not surprisingly, Senator Gale McGee, of Wyoming, who knows the Casper area and the land of the wintering eagles well, waited only long enough to obtain a laboratory diagnostic report on the cause of death before calling a special session of his Subcommittee on Agriculture, Environmental, and Consumer Protection of the Committee on Appropriations. The hearings were conducted in Washington in early June of 1971.[3]

In the minds of the professionals within the United States Bureau of Sport Fisheries and Wildlife, one of the big unanswered questions was what lethal agent had been employed to kill the eagles. Most of the dead eagles were shipped at once to the sprawling Patuxent Wildlife Research Center in Maryland, where the Bureau of Sport Fisheries and Wildlife employs a series of tests to identify poisons in body tissues. Some of the dead eagles were spirited off by state officers at the order of Governor Stanley K. Hathaway to be tested locally as an exercise in states rights. There were several possibilities: The eagles were first tested for sodium fluoroacetate, commonly known as compound 1080, a chemical widely used throughout the West in official government programs of pest and rodent control. The eagles did not show evidence of 1080. They were likewise checked for strychnine, also commonly used in coyote-killing programs in Western sheep country; the response was negative. Next they were tested for cyanide; again the response was negative. This reduced the list of probable lethal agents to the most devastating killer of all.

In 1920 two German chemists had introduced a potent new rodenticide, believed to be a boon to man in his age-old efforts to kill off all the creatures of the earth not directly beneficial to him in some obvious manner. Chemically it was known as thallium sulfate. Tests proved that thallium sulfate, ingested even in minute quantities by birds or mammals, induced a lengthy list of frightening physical failures, including kidney damage, congestion of the lungs, hemorrhage in the gastrointestinal tract, neurologic lesions, and degeneration of the heart and liver, with a lingering death finally coming from a combination of paralysis of the respiratory system, disruption of the blood circulatory system, and—time and breath permitting—pneumonia.

Symptoms of thallium sulfate poisoning may not surface for several hours after the poison is ingested. Within a few days the animal may be suffering paralysis, blindness, deafness, and severe muscular pains. The victim that ingests too little of the poison to die from it may still suffer irreversible brain damage.

Also known to the toxocologists is the fact that thallium sulfate can poison by contact with the skin or by being breathed into the system. In addition, it can poison any terrestrial vertebrates that might feed on the initial victims. Thallium has claimed its share of human victims, the most publicized perhaps being six Mexican laborers who died of thallium poisoning in California in 1932 after eating tortillas made with barley treated with the poison and intended for rodent control. So powerful are the lethal qualities of thallium sulfate that one gram will kill a 150-pound man.

By 1924 this poison had come to the United States and been adopted by federal government field men, who spread it widely over Western states for many years, first for rodent control, then as a general predator control agent. But because of the extreme hazards involved in using this broad-spectrum lethal agent, the government poisoners had used little of it for at least 15 years prior to the Jackson Canyon tragedy.

The report from Patuxent, as well as the Wyoming state agency testing some of the poisoned eagles, brought a uniform verdict. The tests showed 1080 negative, strychnine negative, cyanide negative, evidence of physical damage none; but every eagle except one, which was probably shot, carried from 14 to 152 parts per million of thallium sulfate in its tissues.

Now that the federal agents knew what they were looking for, they wanted to know where the birds had picked it up and how much more there might be lying out on the open range. Federal investigators consulted manufacturers who supply thallium for use in manufacturing rodent control compounds. One manufacturer, the American Smelting and Refining Company, gave them the dates of six thallium sales in Wyoming, five of them in the vicinity of Natrona County, where the eagles had died, and the names of the purchasers, who had paid $10 a pound for quantities ranging from 5 to 25 pounds. Agents rushed to the ranches of these thallium buyers, explained the deadly nature of the substance, and asked that any bait still out in the range be picked up at once and buried deeply along with unused remainders of the poison. All the ranchers agreed. There was little else the agents could do. The ranchers had broken no law by trying to kill coyotes, but the agents were appalled by the rates at which the ranchers had laced the carcasses of bait sheep with thallium. One had used 25 pounds where 3 pounds would have been the lethal dosage as administered by a more experienced predator killer. Another had sacrificed twelve sheep and buried 9½ pounds of thallium in the carcasses; 12 ounces would have been the dosage had it been administered by a professional.[4]

Citizens across the country were demanding that slaughtering of the eagles be halted. In the West there was bitter resentment against the ranchers who had taken the predator control business into their own hands, thereby bringing a deluge of unfavorable publicity on the state. Signs and bumper stickers appeared along the highways of Wyoming: "Watch for Falling Eagles." "Make Sheep the National Bird."[5]

Meanwhile, the wildlife workers were looking repeatedly at their maps. There was something wrong with the puzzle. The pieces were not where they should be. The closest ranch to which they had traced the thallium was 50 miles from Jackson Canyon, and the biologists realized that the eagles out hunting might range only half that distance from their Jackson Canyon roosts. Somewhere closer there must be other ranchers setting out poisoned meat, and these poison stations could be anywhere across hundreds of square miles of open range. Bureau investigators acquired a helicopter and a fixed-wing aircraft, and the search began. "We flew 350 square miles right on the deck," Charles Lawrence later told a congressional committee, "looking for dead animals that might be baited." Among the dead creatures they discovered were sheep, cattle, and deer, which was not particularly unusual. But on their third day, 12 miles from Jackson Canyon, Bureau workers Tom Hutchinson and Norm Johnson saw from their aircraft the remains of three antelope, all lying in the brush along a 2-mile stretch of seldom-used ranch lane near a formation of high, jagged rocks where eagles often perch to rest during the day.

Samples of tissues from the antelope were quickly flown to Denver, where the Bureau laboratory was asked for a speedy report. All three of the antelope carcasses were heavily dosed with thallium.[6]

This was of special interest to the Wyoming Game and Fish Commission, because the antelope had obviously been illegally killed and left in the field. Federal agents, questioning ranchers, worked their way down to one believed responsible for the poisoned-bait stations. Two months before Bruce Wampler and Gordon Krause found the first poisoned eagles in Jackson Canyon, a rancher, his son, two employees, and two other men had gone out in three pickup trucks armed with high-powered rifles. Their purpose was to avenge the deaths that coyotes had supposedly brought to the rancher's sheep. Investigation brought out that, in spite of the closed season on antelope, the gunners brought down eleven of them and proceeded to lace them with thallium. Among the gunners was a former federal employee experienced in rodent control work, who supervised the poison application.

Two or three days later, according to the interrogation, some of this group participated in another antelope hunt during which they are said to have killed nine more head, then placed poison in them. Three of these animals are the ones believed to have been those discovered by the flying federal agents.

A former president of the Wyoming Stockgrowers Association, rancher Van Irvine, was confronted with twenty-nine state charges, while four associates faced a total of seventy-five state charges, including killing antelope out of season and leaving the meat in the field illegally. If given maximum penalties, the offenders might have faced fines totaling more than $10,000. Irvine, pleading *nolo contendere,* insisted on accepting sole responsibility, an act leading the local county attorney to view his action as noble and publicly express admiration and respect for Irvine in the affair. Penalties handed to Irvine were the absolute minumum, $675 plus $4 in court costs.

This was the penalty assessed for an act which had, whether by error or intention, as Alexander Sprunt IV, of the National Audubon Society, told a committee of Congress, ". . . wiped out essentially all of the normal wintering population of bald eagles along that section of the North Platte River in the vicinity of Casper." Others pointed out that federal wool subsidies on his holdings had brought Irvine nearly $100,000 the previous year.[7]

Many of the large sheep ranchers considered the highly publicized episode regretful, less because of the death of the eagles than the fact that the loss had been discovered. Almost certainly such losses of wildlife had gone on previously and involved far more eagles than anyone knew. Nor is there any reason to believe that the attitudes against eagles changed with the publicity surrounding the tragedy of Jackson Canyon. Certainly not all livestock men, even all sheep producers, are eagle haters. Some have learned that eagles are not the everlasting death threat to their sheep and lambs that they have been accused of being. But investigators have found that those least likely to condemn the eagles, or even coyotes, as threats to their economic survival are the smaller operators, the ranchers with little money to buy poisons and to hire pilots or range workers to carry out private predator control campaigns even if they chose to do so. The major predator haters among the sheepmen are the ranchers with big spreads, men with large flocks ranging on public lands as well as private. "Many of the old barons," wrote Tom Bell, editor of the *High Country News,* a highly respected ecologically oriented newspaper published in Lander, Wyoming, "still see themselves as ruler of all they survey, including your land and mine, and all the things thereon—including God's eagles."[8]

Even those who insist that eagles kill large numbers of lambs seldom can recall when they themselves observed such an act of predation. A club limited to those who have witnessed the actual killing of a lamb by an eagle would be an exclusive organization. There have, understandably, been frequent observations of eagles eating sheep. Too often such sightings are followed by a fast leap to the conclusion that the birds killed the animals.

In 1970, according to federal and state agricultural agencies, Wyoming lost 200 adult sheep and 8,400 lambs to eagles. These startling figures deserve careful thought on the basis of some obvious questions.

First, whose figures are these? Unless the sources of

raw data inspire confidence, the conclusions automatically merit suspicion—and in this case the figures are compiled from reports voluntarily mailed in by sheep ranchers. The United States Department of Agriculture each year circulates a questionnaire to ranchers to obtain material for the Wyoming Cooperative Crop and Livestock Reporting Service. Ranchers filling out these forms and returning them to the government are on their honor.

There are some ranchers who do not return the questionnaires. Almost certainly, however, those who hate predators and are convinced that predators should be eliminated use the forms as a tool to maximize their losses. They do not underestimate. The reports that come back are totaled, and the totals are extended to arrive at a figure said to represent the predator losses for the whole state. These maximum figures have served as one justification for the Division of Wildlife Services when making out its annual budget request for its wildlife control programs.

One day at the peak of the public resentment about the dead eagles of Jackson Canyon, my friend Richard McCutchen, a Columbus, Ohio, conservationist, stopped in to tell me about the comparisons he had been making between the sheep in Wyoming and Ohio. In Ohio, although sheep raising is a sizable industry, sheep are, as Dick said, "practically raised in the back yard, instead of out on the open range where they can wander off and get lost. Besides there are no predators working Ohio lambs except for domestic dogs." He had also learned from livestock disease specialists that sheep in Ohio and Wyoming suffer from the same diseases and parasites. "You would think then," he said, "with all those predators they claim in Wyo-

ming, their lamb losses would be much higher than ours."
Then he laid out the following statistics gleaned from the
1970 reports of the United States Department of Agriculture:

	LAMBS BORN	LAMB DEATHS	PERCENTAGE LOSS
Wyoming	1,115,000	129,000	11.57
Ohio	473,000	55,000	11.63

The lamb losses for Ohio and Wyoming are not only
at about the same level but also near the national average
of 11.4 percent of the lamb crop lost to all causes. These
figures indicate to some observers that sheepmen, seeking
additional subsidies for a wobbly industry, channel a large
number of losses from all causes into the predator column,
perhaps hoping to gain tax advantages or to create the
illusion that a more extensive government predator control
program is needed.

One should then take a careful look at the most basic
question; do eagles really eat lambs? Both golden and bald
eagles are quick to spot carrion from their sky-high observation points, and they feed on sheep dead from whatever
cause, ranging from stillbirth to starvation. Ranchers who
claim losses to eagles ignore the results of numerous scientific investigations. As controversy mounted across the
country following the Jackson Canyon slaughter, the National Audubon Society distributed the results of four
scientific studies aimed at determining the real relationship
of eagles to sheep. One was the pioneering Audubon study
already mentioned, which was conducted by Dr. Walter R.
Spofford in Texas in 1963. He had found that ranchers

tend to overestimate the numbers of eagles. He also learned that the prime food of eagles in the Trans-Pacos region of Texas consists of jackrabbits and other rodents, which compete with sheep for the limited grass.

Testimony also came from Montana. There, graduate student Jerry McGahan, studying under Dr. John Craighead, a recognized eagle authority, had collected eagle pellets at thirty-eight nests of the golden eagle across 1,260 square miles of southern Montana's foothills, which are not unlike the rangeland around Casper, Wyoming. Again analysis of the pellets proved that 80 percent of the food of the eagles had been rabbits, especially the white-tailed jackrabbit. Particularly, McGahan had concentrated on one area in the heart of highly productive sheep country, where 18,000 lambs were produced. There he collected eagle pellets containing the remains of 702 individual prey animals, and not one of these items had come from a sheep. Biologist Leo G. Heugly, of the Colorado Cooperative Wildlife Research Unit at Colorado State University, had gone back to Texas, where Dr. Spofford had studied the eagles, purposely to see if he could catch marauding eagles in the act of destroying domestic sheep. He worked on west Texas ranches for three lambing seasons, spending more than 1,100 hours spying on the eagles. During those hours he failed to witness a single instance of an eagle killing a sheep or lamb.[9]

Biologist John Beecham, at work on his master's thesis, spent two years studying the eating habits of the golden eagles of southwestern Idaho. Traveling into remote and lonely valleys, he studied the evidence in and around sixty-one eagle eyries and collected 483 exhibits, the remains of creatures carried by the eagles to their nests. Seventy percent of the food consisted of jackrabbits; among the remainder of the food items there was not one from any domestic creature.

Still another study in the sheep country of west Texas led to the conclusion that eagles could be properly blamed for no more than 0.3 percent of the lamb losses.

With the eagle exonerated—at least for those who believe in factual investigation—one might ask if the other predators could be as devastating as the livestock industry claims. Perhaps even that archdevil, the coyote, the object of hundreds of thousands of dollars' worth of poisoning, trapping, shooting, and denning, might in reality be less the hazard to livestock than his accusers insist. One wonders whether Wyoming actually suffered the loss of 95,000 lambs reported killed there in 1969 by coyotes, and whether Colorado, Montana, or Idaho suffered all their claimed losses to predators for the same year.

In the summer of 1971, a team of fourteen investigators from the University of Michigan's Predator Ecology Laboratory moved into Routt National Forest in northwestern Colorado, where sheepmen graze about 2,500 animals under permit. Throughout the summer months, when sheep are in the high country, the study team kept the flocks under observation day and night, to determine if predators, especially coyotes, caused economically crippling losses to the owners. "Our biological data," reported Sander Orent, project leader, "suggests that widespread and high predator depredations do not in fact occur." This study team failed to locate any sheepmen suffering really severe economic losses from predators, and concluded, according to Orent's report, "that these are rare occurrences."[10] Not everyone across the West wants to see the predators eliminated. Cattlemen often told Orent they like to see and hear the coyotes, which they consider allies against the grass-eating rodents. The small-scale sheep ranchers harbored no great malice toward the coyotes, and often objected to wide-scale efforts to poison the range against predators, preferring instead the occasional removal of the individual predator known to be a problem. Again the coyote haters were found to be primarily the big sheep producers, still insisting that blanket indiscriminate predator killing is essential if they are to stay in business.

In 1970 the Division of Wildlife Services spread an admitted 10,800 baits using the highly lethal and non-specific 1080, plus 805,000 strychnine baits, and 32,933 cyanide "coyote getters." In the face of the long-recognized destruction of nontarget wildlife, the federal government went on year after year, using funds from both federal and local sources to finance the work of its wildlife poisoners, driven by strong pressure from a livestock industry that sees the Western lands, public and private, as the rightful domain of sheep barons and cattle kings. They envision a simplified ecosystem with its living species counted on the fingers of one hand—grass, sheep, cattle, horse, ranchman. Dispensable in this syndrome are all the diverse native wild creatures, beginning with the bison and the black-footed ferret, and ending with the singing coyote and the last of the soaring eagles.

By killing eagles wholesale where the rotting bodies could be detected, the sheepmen dealt their old partner in the slaughter of wildlife, the Washington-based Division of

Wildlife Services, a crippling blow. Confronted by mounting public indignation, both Congress and the executive branch of the federal government became sensitive to the plight of the coyote and the eagle. An advisory committee composed of noted wildlife authorities recommended to the President's Council on Environmental Quality that the nation's long-time program of predator killing should be drastically redesigned and trimmed, and suggested specific methods for accomplishing this end.[11]

No one knows how many wild creatures, innocent or guilty, have perished over the decades because stockmen and the government trappers viewed them as enemies. No one has ever weighed, with confidence in his calculations, the total effect of this wildlife killing on the eventual fate of the vanishing eagles, but uncounted eagles have fallen. I once asked an administrative officer in the Division of Wildlife Services in Washington how many eagles his agency had killed. Looking shocked at the question, he replied, "We don't kill eagles. I hope you are kidding." I was not. The truth is that the agency has killed eagles as the unintentional victims of poison aimed at coyotes and other predators. A dead eagle is equally dead whether killed purposely or not.

This was emphasized by the Audubon Society's Alexander Sprunt IV as he told a Senate subcommittee that the poisoning in Jackson Canyon was "only the tip of the iceberg. During the past decades in which I have been personally involved with eagles, we have heard repeatedly . . . from all over the western United States of the deaths of eagles due to poison baits which are placed for animal control of one kind or another. These deaths are hard to verify, but a number of cases have been investigated and the cause of death determined by the Bureau of Sport Fisheries and Wildlife." Far more eagle deaths from this cause have surely gone undetected. Sprunt made it clear that any compilation of eagle killers had to include the government's predator control agents.[12]

In a warning to his field men, one regional supervisor of the Division of Wildlife Services urged them to take greater care with the placement of poison bait stations to avoid "embarrassment to the Bureau" as a result of killing eagles. "Such eagles," he explained, "are reported immediately to the public." Proving that he was more concerned about bad publicity than dead eagles, he insisted that the answer was patience, and warned that agents should wait to put out their 1080 stations until "tourists, rock hounds, fishermen, hikers, hunters, and picnickers have ceased visiting such areas."[13]

Sheepmen, faced with the president's ban on poison on government lands, were not inclined to reform and stop spreading lethal agents on the range. Governor Hathaway of Wyoming responded to the stockmen by announcing that the state would conduct its own predator control program: "We cannot live in this state without some control of the coyote."[14] Sheepmen, bitter about the government action, began planning their own home-grown variety of poisoning campaigns, and this spectre is a reality which the soaring eagles of the Western states must still face as they scan the land below them for signs of food. Down there on the range the dead antelope or lamb may be an invitation to death, purposely placed in plain view by state agents or privately employed ranch hands.

During the Christmas season following the Jackson Canyon mass eagle poisoning, the Audubon Society conducted its annual Christmas bird count. From the Murie Audubon Society in Casper, Wyoming, came the information that in the Emigrant Gap area, where 14 bald and 53 golden eagles had been found the previous year, spotters could now find only 8 bald and 9 golden eagles.

12

Shotguns and Helicopters

WHEN Charles Lawrence left Dulles International Airport on the morning of May 3, 1971, on his way to investigate the poisoned eagles of Jackson Canyon, he had no way of knowing that he would soon be investigating an eagle massacre of far greater proportions. Nathaniel Reed, on the strength of the news relayed by Charles Callison, had dispatched Lawrence to Wyoming with little advance warning, instructing him to take personal command and investigate the eagle poisoning.

Lawrence was then at the head of the federal government's force of game management agents around the country, a total of about 155 law enforcement specialists who are typically combination policemen, life-long outdoorsmen, and public conscience on wildlife protection. Lawrence's men were thinly spread across the country; many places, Wyoming included, had but a single federal game officer for the entire state. The seriousness of the eagle slaughter uncovered in Wyoming prompted Lawrence to call in a small force of field men from other states to aid in the investigation.

In Wyoming, he soon began to hear almost unbelievable hints of other callous human attacks on eagles, involving far greater losses of birds than those discovered in Jackson Canyon. The morning following his arrival in Casper, Wyoming, Lawrence met with a few stalwarts from the Murie Audubon Society, whose members had been the first to report the gruesome Jackson Canyon discovery. Although Lawrence had flown west to investigate the poisonings, one Audubon worker continued to speak to Lawrence of a persistent rumor around Casper that dead eagles had been seen stacked up along the driveway on a local sheep ranch in the vicinity of Rawling. "His thinking," Lawrence later told me in his Washington office, "was that these eagles had been shot from aircraft, and this was of particular interest to us, because it would be an obvious federal offense." It would differ from the poisoning case in one important detail: there was no way, in view of the wording of the law, that federal officers could make a case on the thallium poisoning because the target may have been coyotes and they could not prove "willful intent" to kill eagles. Investigators from Senator McGee's committee had earlier heard similar reports of the shootings but dismissed them as the kind of talk that "floats around bars on Saturday nights."[1]

Lawrence, the law man, chose to check out the rumors, and called in two of his crack investigators, federal game agents Dale Horne and Willard E. Ritter, who flew into Wyoming and spent the next two months unraveling the skein of rumors and piecing the strange story together. It was soon obvious that a number of prominent ranchers were involved. Paradoxically, some traced the shooting to a bold action taken on March 6, 1970, by then Secretary of the Interior Walter J. Hickel in his efforts to protect the eagles.

Hickel found on his desk one day the usual request from Governor Hathaway of Wyoming asking for the customary permit to kill eagles in countywide areas in Wyoming during 1970. There was nothing new or unusual in the request. Instead of complying, however, Secretary Hickel astounded Western governors by denying the anticipated blanket permits. His reason was simply that the eagles needed protection. Instead of mass death sentences for eagles, the governors were advised that permits would be issued only for the killing of individual eagles—and only if federal agents determined, after an investigation on the scene, that such birds might really be destroying stock. Even if the permits had been issued, federal law would have made shooting eagles from aircraft illegal.

When word of this new decision from Washington flashed across the rangelands, some sheep ranchers, as if under siege by the eagles, promptly moved to institute their own predator control campaigns. Those grazing stock on public lands had signed the customary agreements promising that they would not engage in "do it yourself" predator control work but instead would rely on the services of federal predator control agents. The thallium poisoning was believed traceable in part to reaction to the Hickel ruling, as were the cases of eagle shooting which Lawrence's agents soon began uncovering.

As ranchers in the Trans-Pecos region of Texas had discovered, aircraft are deadly machines for pursuing wild creatures on land or in the air. This was recognized by Doyle Vaughan, who managed the Buffalo Flying Service at Buffalo, Wyoming. The service owned two helicopters, said to be well suited to the grisly business of hunting down and shooting eagles, coyotes, and other wild animals. One of Vaughan's employees was James O. Vogan, a former World War II fighter pilot from Murray, Utah. Vogan had logged more than 4,000 hours in helicopters and 12,500 hours in fixed-wing aircraft. At the age of 48 he was a licensed airline transport pilot, qualified to fly several kinds of aircraft, including helicopters, and to instruct in the flying of both helicopters and fixed-wing aircraft.

In the autumn of 1970 Vogan was dispatched, with a helicopter, to the ranch of Herman Werner, near Casper, Wyoming. The same Herman Werner was father-in-law to Van Irvine, who was involved in the thallium poisoning. Vogan testified that his assignment was to fly the rangeland and kill predators, for which Buffalo Flying Service was to be paid a flat fee, with each dead eagle worth $25.[2]

Vogan, as pilot, did not customarily perform the actual executions. His hands were full maneuvering the helicopter to keep his gunner in range of the birds as the eagles attempted to escape. The seat beside him was always occupied by a gunner carrying a twelve gauge shotgun loaded with 3-inch magnums. On some occasions the gunner would be an employee of the Buffalo Flying Service. But ordinarily Vaughan could obtain free help by finding gunners around town or on the ranches, where there always seemed to be someone eager to go along and do the shooting.

"Did he pay the gunners?" Senator McGee asked. "Why would the others go out and freeze their fingers and feet?"

"For the enjoyment of it," Vogan replied. He also testified that invariably the gunners were told that the operation was covered by permits making it legal for them to kill eagles.[3]

Depending on the distance to their shooting areas and how long the men could hold out against the sometimes bitter cold, the helicopter flights lasted from one to two hours. On some days there would be three flights. Vogan reports that the bald eagle, more capable of tricky maneuvering than the golden, proved far more difficult to shoot down. "The Golden Eagle, I would say, is not really a hard bird to zero in on and get your gunner in position to shoot, but a Bald Eagle, if you shoot a Bald Eagle down, I can guarantee you, you earn your money." Vogan testified that he had, "seen as high as a box of shells shot up on one eagle." He found the eagle to be a "tough bird," and added that, "even if they look dead, you had better get out and kick them and make sure, and you better have a gun or something to protect yourself."

Word of this mass bounty hunting might not have leaked out except that some of the gunners, perhaps still believing themselves to be law-abiding eagle killers, shooting under permit, frequently went into town and shared accounts of their flying experiences with acquaintances.

Common rumor had it also that some of the eagles had been shot across the state line in Colorado. That state's conservation officers were believed to have flown observation flights over the helicopter but failed to observe the actual shooting of eagles.

As the shooting continued, the ranchers became increasingly cautious. They began hiding the dead eagles in graves. In the early stages they had demanded that Vogan land and bring in his dead eagles as proof. Some of these were the birds apparently seen stacked up. Later they were moved and buried. Finally, Vogan was instructed not to bring eagles back to ranch headquarters, but to leave them where they fell. There was a growing uneasiness, a suspicion that federal agents were becoming interested.

Vogan was convinced that if the federal agents did move in, the ranchers and Vaughan, not the pilot, would be the first to know about it. "They would have thrown the whole blame on me," Vogan said. He was beginning to feel that "somebody was going to get hung in the tree." At this point Vogan contacted Senator Gale W. McGee, seeking immunity and offering, in exchange, to give full testimony before a congressional committee. This did not mean that Vogan had acquired any new concern for the welfare of the vanishing eagles. He saw the eagles as destructive predators. Even when he was not supposed to be killing eagles, Vogan admitted that he had sometimes put his gunners in range of the big birds, apparently believing it the proper thing to do in the interest of his clients.

During his hearings before Senator McGee's committee in Washington, August 2 and 3, 1971, Vogan unraveled an almost unbelievable story of destruction of an endan-

gered wildlife resource. The figures he recited were charac-
terized by Nathaniel Reed, assistant secretary of the interior, as "absolutely sickening statistics."

After telling of how they had the dead eagles stacked
up, Vogan brought forth his pocket notebook in which he
had recorded after each flight the total killed. On November 18, 1970, his records showed that he arrived at the
Bolton Ranch, owned by Herman Werner, and in his first
afternoon his gunner downed one eagle and also killed six
coyotes. Vogan continued to read the wildlife obituaries
from his little notebook:

Ten eagles and two coyotes.

Nine eagles and one coyote.

Two eagles and two coyotes.

Seven eagles and three coyotes.

Fourteen eagles and no coyotes.

The body count droned on, flight after flight, day after
day, through more than six months of what must rank as
one of the most concentrated local efforts in recent times
to destroy eagles. The best days for the gunners, according
to Vogan, were windy days, when eagles would leave their
perches and soar effortlessly on the updrafts. By the time
one bird was shot from the sky the next victim was often
already in view. One day Vogan and his gunner killed 29
eagles, another day 31, and on one especially rewarding
day, 36 of the giant birds. As he flew, Vogan tried to
remember his score until he landed and could make a hurried entry in his notebook: "We were shooting so many

down it would be almost impossible to keep track of them from memory."

There was good reason for writing down the kill. This was the talley sheet by which his employer collected his executioner's fees: $50 per coyote and $25 per eagle, supposedly deductible from taxes as a business expense. The rate for eagles was the same whether bald or golden.

In all probability the final count of dead eagles from this operation will never be precisely known. Vogan might have forgotten one or two in the heat of the chase. "Well, I kept a record up to a certain point, and I kept a record in my own mind of the eagles that were killed, and I estimated or had a count in my own mind of 570 alone on the Bolton Ranch and around 200 on the other ranches."

In addition to eagles and coyotes, wildlife shot during these aerial gunning missions admittedly included several Canada geese, antelope, deer, bobcats, several elk—of which Vogan was allowed one—and a bear shot by Vogan's 11-year-old son.

For its predator killing services, Werner is believed to have paid Buffalo Flying Service at least $15,000. Vogan took considerable pride in the fact that Werner did not question his body count figures and added that the rancher had driven out in his station wagon and watched him killing eagles part of the time. Werner later hired Vogan to pilot his own aircraft, although he denied that Vogan had been given instructions to kill eagles.[4]

Evidence gathered during the federal investigation offered, as Nathaniel Reed had predicted, a "sordid story," showing "cold, callous, deliberate defiance of Federal and State law."[5]

The tip about a cache of dead eagles on the Werner ranch had prompted Everett L. Sutton, United States regional supervisor of the Division of Management and Enforcement in Albuquerque, to dispatch two men and a truck carrying a backhoe. They made their way from Colorado up to Wyoming and were standing by when needed. At the time the search warrant was served on Herman Werner, the excavating equipment was approaching the ranch. The grave was located and the digging soon brought up what Sutton described to me as "a mass of rotting eagle bones and feathers."

The rumors heard by Lawrence upon his arrival in Casper eventually brought the key figures named in Vogan's testimony into federal and state courts. There is little agreement among judges as to how society should penalize a person for knowingly and willfully killing an eagle in these days when the big birds are a subject of national concern. In the fall of 1972 Doyle Vaughan came to trail before United States District Court Judge Ewing T. Kerr in Cheyenne, Wyoming, charged with 374 counts: 366 for killing eagles, 7 for killing Canada geese, and 1 for conspiracy. He was allowed to plead guilty to 74 counts of eagle killing and the conspiracy charge. Charges for killing the other 292 eagles were dismissed. The federal law has been strengthened since the offense was committed, but at the time of the shooting the penalty on the 74 counts of eagle killing could have brought Vaughan a maximum sentence of 37 years in jail plus fines up to $37,000. His total penalty, however, was $500 (the maximum for one eagle) and 6 months of unsupervised probation.[6]

Whether privately done or carried out as government

policy, the bounty system has proved to make poor sense both biologically and economically. Consider the bounty-hunting history of Alaska over those prolonged years when Alaskans killed a variety of creatures, eagles included, because officials levied a price on their heads. Following the gold rush years the rise of commercial salmon fishing, then the fox fur industry, brought new demands to kill off Alaska's predators. Together, the salmon fishermen and the fur producers made their voices heard in the territorial legislature in Juneau, and in 1917 Alaska established a bounty on the bald eagle. For every pair of eagle claws turned in, Alaska would reward the hunter with 50 cents. In the years that followed, hunters and trappers living in isolated cabins in the forests and along the coves supplemented meager incomes by killing eagles. Stores placed signs in their windows announcing that they accepted eagle claws in exchange for flour, beans, and boots. Increasingly the idea of such bounties became firmly fixed in the lives and minds of the Alaskan people.

At least one bounty hunter I heard of was careful not to shoot out the adult birds but to take his toll from the immatures, thereby leaving seed stock to keep himself in business. But the more common practice, as related to me by Doug Richmond, a former eagle hunter who became soured on the profession, was to cruise the shorelines while watching the distant treetops for the perching eagles. "I was rather a successful hunter," said Richmond. "I can remember one day when I killed seventeen eagles by three in the afternoon, and that was by no means an above-average day."

By 1923 Alaska was paying $1 per eagle, and in 1949,

with passage of a new bounty act, Alaska's price on the head of the bald eagle rose to $2. And the bounty hunting continued in spite of the fact that elsewhere the killing of bald eagles had been outlawed by federal regulation since 1940. In 1952 federal protection of the bald eagle extended at last to the birds of Alaska, thus bringing to an end the eagle bounty system. From 1917 through 1952, Alaska had paid $133,042.50 to its citizens as rewards for killing 128,273 bald eagles.[7]

No one can say for certain what effect bounty hunting may have had on the bald eagle populations of Alaska. It seems likely that bounty hunting alone may not have reduced the populations permanently. But there were, at the same time, other forces working against the eagles, and whether the falling salmon supply, deforestation, and invasion of the wilderness by people, all combined with the persistent bounty killing, might have permanently altered the eagle population levels we can never know with certainty.

We do know, however, that the larger predators can be eliminated from the earth by persistent overkill. The wolf, the grizzly bear, and the cougar, are all in serious trouble through most of their range, and all are large creatures at the tops of their food chains, creatures which, like the eagle, have a lower biotic potential than smaller animals farther down their food chains. Such creatures are the ones the predator hunters have been able to remove from the fauna with the greatest success.

Campaigns carried out against remnants of endangered species, as in the case of the Wyoming eagles, are a monumental threat. Every individual animal taken from the population reduces the chances for that species to survive. In sheep country, where coyote control on a general broad spectrum may not reduce the coyotes more than temporarily, the same program, if it feeds poison to eagles, is capable of incalculable harm.

With regard to those Western stockmen using the public range the question seems clear enough. Why should the federal government continue to hand ridiculously cheap grazing rights and subsidies to those who prove their poor stewardship by destroying any part of the federal property they use? The rancher privileged to graze his animals on the people's land owns neither the land nor any of the resources on it except the blades of grass as they are consumed by his animals. The wild creatures of the public land belong, not to the rancher, but to all the citizens of the United States. The birds flying above the land, and living from it, are federal or state property. No part of an ecosystem can be destroyed or removed without affecting the vitality of the whole. The eagles and the coyotes cannot be taken away without diminishing the value of the public property. The privilege to graze should carry a moral and legal responsibility to maintain the public land in perpetuity. It follows that the stockman who abuses that privilege should lose his right to dominant use of that public property.

The validity of this principle was recognized by the members of the "Cain Committee," the Advisory Committee on Predator Control, reporting in 1971 to the Council on Environmental Quality. This blue-ribbon study group flatly recommended that any grazing permit be revoked if the stockman holding the permit was guilty of illegally taking wildlife, whether the offense occurred on his own property or the public domain. "The case is clear," stated the report, "when permit holders carry on such practices on federal land. It seems to us to be equally applicable when a permit holder is convicted of such violations on private land. . . . Such livestock producers are not responsible permit holders."[8]

The big Wyoming eagle shooting fest was all-out war against the eagles, and the body count indicated an astounding disregard for the laws of man and the rights of the eagle. There was no denying that the admissions of Vogan before the congressional committee shocked the country, and that the expressions of disgust were genuine. Nor was the condemnation of the eagle killing limited to the old line conservation groups whose reaction could be anticipated. In recent times there has been an awakening among Americans to the plight of many of the wild species with which we share the earth. People take note when an eagle is shot today.

Late in the summer of 1963 a little group of bird watchers from London, Ontario, drove out to see an eagle nest that had been reported to them. While they stood looking at the adult through their binoculars, they heard the sharp crack of a rifle and the eagle tumbled from the nest tree and fell to the ground dead. The surprised poacher was caught by the bird watchers and promptly taken to court.

In Knoxville, Tennessee, during the Christmas season of 1971, a vandal went up to the cage where the zoo's bald eagle had lived for 10 years and shot it from its perch. Anger swept the Tennessee city. A few months later, however, there was a replacement in the cage. This was a female brought to the zoo to recover. She too had become locally famous around Reelfoot Lake after being found crippled by lead shot.

In 1971 two of the fifty bald eagles believed then to be living in Maine were found dead of gunshot. Both had been members of breeding pairs.

These are a few of the notorious eagle shooters, the ones we hear about, and—even including such mass slaughter as described by James Vogan—they are the tip of the iceberg. Eagles are still shot, some from the air, others one at a time as they swoop low across a duck marsh or glide past a farmhouse, and they are left hidden in the brush unseen and uncounted.

"We must recognize," said Russell E. Train, Chairman of the Council on Environmental Quality, before a committee of Congress, "that although the number of eagles already found dead [from shooting and poison] is distressingly large, in all probability this number only represents a part of the total toll. In rough and extensive terrain, such as the part of Wyoming in which the dead birds have been discovered, it is likely that only a part of the total number of birds which have been killed will be found."[9]

13

Land of Many Eagles

WHEN Fred Robards leaves his family in Juneau, Alaska, and goes off in search of the bald eagles, he eases his official work boat, the *Surfbird,* out of the narrow harbor into wild and wooded valleys as beautiful and lonely as any in North America. The rivers and bays are rich with salmon of five species and schools of herring that make the cold waters foam; at low tide crabs and clams are in the shallows, and abalone are found clinging to the rocks. This Alaskan wilderness is eagle country.

Ragged timbered shorelines sweep upward from sea level to snowy peaks of 4,000 feet or more. Southeast Alaska is the site of the Tongas National Forest, largest of all the nation's 154 official timberlands. The Tongas, covering 16 million acres, is a land of steep-walled valleys, glaciers, snow-capped peaks, and thousands of rushing ice water streams that carry the rains and snow-melt into the saltwater fjords. Over all this wild country, up and down the slopes, is spread a lush, dark green rain forest of coniferous giants.[1]

For thousands of years much of this forest has stood untouched by saw and ax, climax forest where the native vegetation reaches its ultimate accommodation with earth and climate. The forests are largely of two kinds of trees. First there are the towering Sitka spruce, their green, pointed tops pushing like spears into the low, scudding clouds. Sitka, the largest spruce in North America, can average 100 feet high or more, and some grow to twice that, gaining at a rate of 2 feet a year. Having reached its maximum height, a Sitka spruce may stand on its mountain-side as a living giant for 800 years or longer, wearing an eagle's nest in its crown.

Where the forest grows dense, the lower branches of the spruce fall away, leaving a dark brown trunk many logs high to tempt the timberman, and only at the top of these forest giants, where there is light, is there still green growth wedging into the sky. Sitka spruce grow in a belt 40 or 50 miles wide along the western coast of North America for 2,000 miles, from Kodiak Island southward to Mendocino County, California.[2]

More abundant than the spruce in some parts of southeast Alaska is the western hemlock, which forms a verdant green jungle, in a climate where rainfall may total 100 inches a year and where soft moist mosses carpet the spongy forest floor, spread along the trees, and blanket the limbs.

Southeast Alaska is a wild land of irregular rocky sea-shores, a rich and productive region where wild creatures abound. The world's biggest bears, weighing 1,000 pounds

or more, live in these forests and come to the edges of the
ocean and the streams to feed on salmon. Giant moose are
here and the little Sitka black-tailed deer, cousin of the
Columbia black-tail. Millions of salmon work their way up
the streams to spawn and die, and bears, gulls, eagles, and
others come to feast on the bodies. Living here also are
wolves, wolverines, martin, fox, otter, beaver, and mink.

In this southeastern section of Alaska where Fred Robards works with the eagles, there are 13,000 miles of
shoreline. One island alone, Admiralty, 100 miles long by
25 miles wide, encompasses 1,665 square miles and has
678 miles of coast. Its streams are world-famous for salmon
and the big brown bears that come to feed on them.[3]

Human communities are small and widely separated
in this wild country, and dwarfed by the grandeur of the
natural scene. There are few roads, power lines, or other
structures to break the wilderness. The little crew of the
Surfbird can work for weeks, alone most of the time except
for the nearby wild creatures.

In his search for eagle nests, Fred Robards is usually
one of a three-man crew. Aboard the 65-foot work boat, in
addition to Robards, is Sid O. Morgan, Game Management
Agent of the United States Bureau of Sport Fisheries and
Wildlife. Morgan grew up fishing and hunting rabbits with
Robards back in the same neighborhood in Washington
State. Also in the crew is Joe Johnson, who has lived for
many years close to the Alaskan wilderness, by fishing,
raising foxes, and even shooting eagles for bounty before
bounty hunting was outlawed in Alaska in 1952. Johnson,
feeling much at home in the lonely coves and channels,
pilots the boat and maintains it while Robards and Morgan

are off scouting for eagle nests from smaller outboard-powered boats carried along for the purpose. Their assignment is simply to locate and map every eagle nest along those thousands of miles of coastline in southeast Alaska, so that the United States Forest Service can inform timber cutters and they can watch for the trees of the eagles and save them from the saw.

Seldom does Robard's little survey miss a nest tree. In one recent year timber cutters operating in southeastern Alaska found only two nests not on Robard's maps. At each of these the crews stopped, reported the eagles, and promptly began to work around the nest tree as the law prescribes. "I think," Robards muses, "people are getting the idea."

During the eagle nest surveys, Robards and Morgan move slowly and methodically. "We can cover about ten miles of shore in a ten-hour day," Robards told me in his office in Juneau. "You get so you can pick out likely eagle trees," Robards says. For Robards this work began in 1966 when, with Bureau of Sport Fisheries and Wildlife pilot-biologist James King, he started investigating the eagle populations of Admiralty Island. "There was a lot we didn't know," Robards says, "eagles had not been studied much in Alaska. We didn't even know how many there might be."[4]

About this time there was evidence that the region might be facing major economic and industrial changes in the early future. Until 1940, logging in Alaska had consisted of small scattered cuts. But now large contracts were being let for timbering for pulp and plywood. Unless the eagle research began soon, and baseline facts were recorded, no one would ever fully understand what the coming changes might mean to the welfare of the bald eagles. By learning all they could about the needs of these birds, they might hopefully save the eagles from the fate they already faced elsewhere on the continent.

King and Robards divided Admiralty Island into eighty-six plots, each with 10 miles of beachline. Next, they made a random sampling of these plots for their census work. They used a small maneuverable float plane and a helicopter, and also worked from water level in their boat. They reworked each test area until they could find no more nests, marking every nest location on the map. Gradually, the eagle counters grew to understand the distribution of the birds. They soon learned that eagles seeking nest trees avoid logged-over areas. Those earliest saws and axes broke age-old bonds between giant birds and giant trees and even as the trees returned, the eagles did not move back to risk new eyries in their crowns. Shorelines logged as much as 60 years earlier were still without eagle nests.

After locating the nests, the biologists later returned and flew the area in a helicopter to count the eagles' eggs. These eagle counts revealed for the first time some important preferences of Alaska's nesting eagles. With a choice between spruce and hemlock, at least 90 percent of the eagles chose the stronger limbs of the Sitka spruce. The biologists also found that all nests were built within a narrow strip of forest along the beaches. Each pair of eagles selects for its nest a tree within 200 yards of the shore. Often the nest trees are on points of land where the watchful eagles command a view both up and down the shore. Every nest, without exception, had this free and unobstructed approach to the waters where the parent eagles hunt.

Until this preliminary study no one had suspected the density of the eagle populations on Admiralty Island. The study plots held an average of 13.3 nests each. When inspected in May, at the peak of the egg-laying season, 5.3 nests per plot were in active use, with a hatching success of 82 percent. Later, when these figures were expanded by accepted statistical methods, Admiralty Island was found to be producing an estimated 648 fledgling eagles for the year. All along these coasts the distances between active nests averaged out at less than 2 miles, and frequently, in the better fishing areas, were even closer.[5]

There was no time to spare in making a complete nest count along all of the coast where timber might soon be cut. The Bureau of Sport Fisheries and Wildlife worked out an agreement with the United States Forest Service, protecting nest trees from cutting and leaving all other trees within 330 feet of such a tree standing, so that each would be a green island where, hopefully, the eagles would continue to nest. At least a year before an area is scheduled for timbering, the Forest Service sends its plan and maps to Robards, and he heads into the wilderness in search of the eagle nests. Each one is marked with yellow plastic "Wildlife Tree" signs, and the Forest Service is supplied with the information.

Finding Admiralty Island's eagle nests was only a beginning: that island, as large as it is, accounts for only 6.5 percent of the coastline in southeastern Alaska. Still to be surveyed were more than 12,000 miles of coves and island shores. By 1971, Robards had mapped the nests along 1,300 miles of this coast. Robards would not hazard a guess as to how much longer it would take him to complete his work. "It looks" he said, "as if I'll be at it a while."

On the basis of the count already taken, Robards and Jim King estimate that there are perhaps 40,000 bald eagles in Alaska with at least 3,800 breeding pairs living in the southeastern part.

Perhaps 2,000 of these live far out in the Aleutian Islands, where there are no forests at all. About 200 islands within this chain, which curves off toward Asia, lie within the Aleutian Islands National Wildlife Refuge, and the largest concentration of eagles in the Aleutians are around 40-mile-long Amchitka Island, lying between the Bering Sea and the Pacific Ocean, 1,400 miles southwest of Anchorage. One winter day on Amchitka I saw seventy eagles from one location. They had congregated to feed on table scraps brought to the dump from an Atomic Energy Commission construction camp then on the island. Since then, the AEC has moved to close its camp, and, of course, the dump which had become the eagle's lunch stand. The eagles have probably spread out again to earn their living around the edge of the sea.

There is at least one place in Alaska with even a larger concentration of bald eagles. Around Haines, 60 miles north of Juneau, one may witness a great eagle spectacular along the Chilkat River. From beneath this river's flood plain, warmer waters percolate and temper the icy Chilkat far into the winter months, so that after other streams in the area are frozen hard and fast, the Chilkat still moves in gurgling open currents between snow-covered banks.

Into this open water the dog salmon move to spawn late in the season, when the salmon run has already ended elsewhere. There the eagles concentrate, beginning in October, and in a single 3-mile length of the Chilkat there may at times be 3,000 eagles fishing in the stream or perched on the nearby cottonwoods. Robards has counted as many as 700 from one place without moving. The numbers vary depending on the supply of fish. Eagles fish a series of broad riffles over which the salmon, spent from spawning, and about to die, drift back downstream. The eagles reach their peak numbers in early December on the Chilkat, and six weeks later there may still be several dozen in the vicinity.

But there is a threat to this winter feeding area, as there seems to be everywhere for the national bird. Beneath this section of the river lies a deposit of iron ore, and Mitsubishi of Japan is negotiating with the Indians of the Klukwan Village to remove the ore from the alluvial fan by strip mining the area from which the upwelling of warm water comes. No one can tell what such a development would mean to eagles that rely on the spent salmon there in early winter, or whether the dust-fine tailings from the mine will ruin the stream as spawning water for salmon.

As the national bird vanishes from other parts of its broad original range, the Alaskan reservoir of eagles becomes a final buffer between the eagles and extinction. Laboratory analysis shows that Alaska's eagles already carry small amounts of DDT and its derivatives in their tissues, as all of us do. But the levels are low enough so that the eagles of Alaska have not yet suffered apparent damage to the hatchability of their eggs. There is still hope that chemical contamination of their environment can be suppressed to save these last of the eagles from the fate of their cousins in Ohio, Maine, and other states of the "lower forty-eight."

But this last land of the eagle is already undergoing change. It does not matter that Alaska is twice the size of Texas and has only half the population of Rhode Island. This once formidable wilderness, always a challenge to bold men, is attracting the attention of industry. The prizes are oil, hard minerals, and timber, and the onslaught is just now beginning. Alaska's geographic isolation, deep-freeze temperatures, and hostile landscape may slow down the forces but can scarcely hope to hold back the tide. The changes will come as surely as the Mendenhall Glacier scars the slopes of its valley. In the face of this, hope lies in learning as much as possible about the needs of the bald eagles, the brown bears, sea otters, and other magnificent wild creatures that are part of the historic Alaskan scene, and in making concessions for them.[6]

As for the eagles which Fred Robards and his crew have watched across so many miles of Alaskan skies, he has one suggestion. Along with other biologists, Robards favors setting aside a buffer strip, a narrow shoreline band of timber to be left standing for the nesting eagles. "It would not have to be wide," says Robards hopefully, "maybe 150 yards from the water would do it. This kind of eagle refuge would be far better than large blocks of forest. Eagles nest close to the water."

14

First Aid and Deep Concern

THERE is a remarkable and growing concern over the impending disappearance of the bald eagle. Perhaps Americans are beginning to feel a sense of guilt as the national bird struggles to survive in a land made increasingly hostile by the acts of man. The species that nearly obliterated the eagle is now remorsefully attempting to rescue it.

One October day in 1971, when Florida Audubon Society member Cliff Head was driving slowly along the Sunshine Parkway, keeping pace with the heavy expressway traffic, he saw a bald eagle struck a glancing blow by one of the speeding cars ahead of him. The crippled bird went out of control immediately, to flounder in the path of approaching traffic. Head, risking his own safety, tramped on the brakes, slid to an abrupt halt, and began backing up against the traffic to where the stunned eagle lay on the expressway.

There he began flagging down other cars and directing them around the scene of the accident. Finally he gathered up the bird and put it into his car, and with an ambulance driver's singleness of purpose raced on toward Maitland and the headquarters of the Florida Audubon Society. Out of somewhere came a State Highway Patrol escort to clear the path.

At the office of the Audubon Society all other business came to a halt. During the following days the eagle received expert care and medical treatment, and, feasting on a diet of dead animals picked up by well-wishers along the highways, plus liberal dosages of vitamin supplements, quickly began to regain its strength.

Nine days after its dramatic rescue the young eagle was released to the wild, while newsmen's cameras recorded the launching. Before its release it was marked with a harmless white paint, and some days later it was seen from the windows of a blimp, fully recuperated and flying free over the pine forests of central Florida.[1]

In at least one notable instance eagles have influenced highway planners. Along the west coast of Florida, where I-75 swings eastward toward Miami, the surveyors found their route blocked by a pine tree 50 feet high. This would have posed only a momentary problem, except that the pine tree held a gigantic occupied eagle nest in its crown. Officials at local, state, and federal levels conferred about the fate of the nest tree. Big yellow machines idled. Finally the question was settled to the satisfaction of all when the highway was rerouted, in a graceful curve, 300 feet to the west. This thoroughfare became perhaps the first interstate highway anywhere to be built around an eagle tree.

Among the stranger stories of concern for the remaining eagles is an account of the troubles confronted by a nesting pair about 40 miles southwest of Cape Kennedy. The tragedy began when an unidentified gunner shot the female eagle with a rifle, breaking a large wingbone and bringing her down among the palmettos, where she was later found by a surveyor.

He called in the Audubon Society, whose members captured the struggling eagle and carried her home to be nursed back to health on hand-fed fish. Meanwhile, the bird believed to be her mate appeared to be sitting on the nest, assuming alone the duties of incubation. How could he take time to leave the nest and hunt for food to assure his survival? His human benefactors promptly arranged for a small plane to carry out twice weekly air drops of fish to be left near the nest. All this sounds wonderfully heartwarming, but the facts became somewhat garbled in the telling. The truth, as later ascertained, is that the nest to which the fish were delivered was not really that of the injured eagle. But the fish perhaps did not go to waste and surely no one can fault the rescue crew on its devotion to purpose.

In another way of aiding the national bird, the National Wildlife Federation launched its own system of bounty payments on eagle shooters. Anyone giving information leading to the arrest and conviction of an eagle killer could claim the federation's $500 reward. As word of this award spread, the federation cheerfully made good on its offer in such cases as that of Gary Buss of Colfax, Wisconsin. Buss, after witnessing the shooting of an immature bald eagle, reported the incident to the United States Bureau of Sport Fisheries and Wildlife. The eagle, which suffered a damaged right wing, was fed and treated for two months until healthy enough to survive again in the wild. It was released amid the abundance of the Necedah National Wildlife Refuge.[2]

Destruction of an eagle nest, even by natural forces, is frequently viewed by people in these times as a catastrophe. The broad, lonely wetlands of the Agassiz National Wildlife Refuge in northern Minnesota is the historic home of a multitude of waterfowl, moose, and assorted other wild creatures, including at one time a few bald eagles. In 1962, a windstorm swept across that flat marsh country and brought to earth a tree that had been used by a nesting pair of eagles for many years. It was the only remaining eagle nest on the refuge, and the manager, surveying the destruction, decided to erect an artificial platform hoping to encourage the pair of eagles, upon their return the following spring, to remain in their old territory.

First, the crew built a metal tower 30 feet high, then constructed a metal frame shaped like a big basket, and belted it to the top of the tower. Into this frame went sticks collected from the eagle's old nest. Finally the nest builders stood back and admired their work, wondering if the birds would accept this substitute eagle tree. A week later an adult bald eagle arrived and was watched hopefully as it perched nearby. The bird studied the structure as if puzzled by what it saw. But for all this effort something was unsatisfactory. Some weeks later the eagles began building a new nest 4 miles away, but after building they departed and did not return and there has not been a nesting pair of bald eagles on Agassiz since 1962.[3]

Eagles, however, vary in nature from one pair to the next, and some years later I heard a more encouraging "nest building" story out of Michigan's lower peninsula. Each year, during their eagle-banding operations, Sergej Postupalsky and his tree-climbing assistant Jack Holt made a midsummer visit to an old productive eyrie to band the young. They arrived one day to find the tree blown down. "The two eagles," Holt recalled, "fell to the ground and by the time we got there, one had been taken by a predator. The other one, however, was still there and the grass around the sassy, hissing eaglet was flattened down where the parent birds had carried food to it."

Holt and Postupalsky built and carried into the forest a wooden pallet 4 feet square, and with the aid of his climbing ropes, Holt wrestled this platform 40 feet into the treetops. There he secured it near where the first nest had stood. Next, he wrapped the eaglet in his jacket and carried it up the tree to place it carefully in the new nest. The parents adapted quickly and continued to feed their young one, perhaps the first case on record of wild bald eagles using an artificial nesting structure. The following season, however, the pair built a new nest 150 yards from their man-made platform.

In addition to nest trees eagles need perches, because they spend much of their time resting. Near Klamath Falls, Oregon, there is a strange structure formed of three 60-foot high Douglas fir poles, like the frame of a giant tepee, erected one bitterly cold weekend by a volunteer crew of forest workers from the Weyerhaeuser Company. It has a single purpose: to provide a perch for the local bald eagles while they rest or study the surrounding lake watching for food. Eagle watchers around town recall that the birds formerly perched in two tall poplar trees, but the aging trees were felled by a combination of working beavers and powerful winds. The plight of the eagles was explained to the foresters, who designed the tower. The first rewards for this pioneering effort came on Christmas morning, when townsfolk discovered a pair of adult bald eagles calmly perched on the top of their new man-made resting structure.[4]

Since early in the 1960s the Florida Audubon Society and landowners have maintained nesting sanctuaries for bald eagles throughout central Florida's ranching country. In this land of pines, palmettos, and hundreds of lakes, large and small, the immediate threats to the eagles included the burning and cutting of nest trees and human interference with nesting. The Audubon workers began searching out the nesting territories and talking with landowners. So many ranchers wanted to help the eagles that over a few years nearly 4 million acres of central Florida were brought into the new Cooperative Bald Eagle Sanctuary plan.[5]

Money was spent for hundreds of printed signs and other expenses, and to support the eagle sanctuary plan the Florida Audubon people went into the stamp-collecting business. Their call went nationwide for donations of stamps, particularly commemorative issues, valued by collectors. People who had seldom thought about the plight of the eagles, or about stamps either, began saving stamps to help the birds. In the Audubon office these stamps are sorted and packed by volunteer workers, then sent off to dealers. The stamp program raises about a thousand dollars a year to keep the eagle sanctuaries in operation.

Government agencies charged with supervision of public lands have instituted programs to protect eagle trees in the national forests, wildlife refuges, national parks, and on holdings under the jurisdiction of the Army Corps of Engineers and the Bureau of Land Management. Such programs not only prohibit the cutting of eagle nest trees or trees near the nest site but also attempt to keep people and vehicles from the vicinity, especially during the critical nesting season. Snowmobiles can be a special scourge in early spring, when the eagles are in the beginning phase of their annual nesting cycle. The nervous birds may abandon their nest if disturbed. There is still snow on the ground in the North Woods, and the machines still roar along the lakes and over the white forest trails. Increasingly, the answer to the problem has been to ban snowmobiles after March 1 from parts of state and national forests where there are known eagle nests.

Timber companies, with their large private holdings, often share responsibility for the protection of eagle nesting areas. In 1967 Boise Cascade, Weyerhaeuser, and the Northern States Power Company, which maintains 30,000 acres of wilderness in Minnesota and Wisconsin, became cooperators with the Bureau of Sport Fisheries and Wildlife in managing their company lands with special consideration for the nesting eagles using their trees. Such policies usually call for locating nest sites, marking them to prevent loggers from cutting nest and perch trees, and creating special nesting-season buffer zones around them. The nest locations are kept secret to shield the nesting eagles from curious human intruders.

Zoo managers are increasingly convinced that their enclosures hold hope for endangered wild species of many kinds. But the sobering truth is that birds of prey have not adapted readily to breeding in captivity. Ages of free flight so conditioned them to courting in the limitless skies that nesting in a cage is not readily nor widely embraced. Seldom has the mighty bald eagle gone through the stages of its breeding cycle while held captive. The earliest record I have found of bald eagles breeding in captivity was reported in *Forest and Stream* in 1887. This account tells of the eagles held by Henry Hulse, a citizen of Toledo, Ohio, who had a love for the birds of prey, eagles in particular.

About the summer of 1880, Hulse robbed the nest of a pair of bald eagles along the western end of Lake Erie near Toledo. Shortly afterwards he acquired two more eagles about the same age. He kept these birds for several years, and eventually all four acquired the gleaming, white heads and tails of mature birds. As good fortune would have it, two of Hulse's eagles were male and two female. In a slatted cage built into the back porch of his home, Hulse installed a nesting box 1 foot deep and 3 feet square. The first chick hatched April 23, 1886, after 35 days of incubation, during which the male dutifully delivered fish to his mate on the nest. The following year Hulse's eagles hatched another young one, this time after an incubation period of 37 days.

Nearly two decades later, at the Buffalo Zoological Gardens, Dr. F. A. Crandall recorded the hatching of six young eagles from birds in the zoo cages between 1906 and 1916.[6]

During the spring of 1971, a pair of white-tailed sea eagles, held in the Swope Park Zoo in Kansas City, Kansas, began courtship displays and nest building. They produced a fertile egg, and to the jubilation of zoo officials, successfully hatched a chick of this nearly extinct species. This news bouyed the hopes of zoo managers everywhere.

Practitioners of falconry are even more convinced than are the zoo keepers that raptors can be reared consistently in captivity. They can point to occasional successes. In New York, Dr. Heinz Meng, Professor of Ornithology at State College in New Paltz, and a falconer with a long-time, consuming interest in peregrine falcons, announced in the summer of 1971 that his peregrines had reared a chick. The following year the performance was repeated. This was a rare and exhilarating accomplishment, and encouraged other falconers to try to bring their captive birds to breed.[7]

Cornell University's Laboratory of Ornithology has instituted a large-scale program aimed at rearing birds of prey. Under the guidance of Dr. Tom J. Cade, Cornell's noted raptor research specialist, the laboratory designed and erected a new "hawk barn." This remarkable building, constructed in late 1970, contains forty large cage areas for housing individual pairs of birds of prey. The structure is equipped with special observation windows of one-way glass. Special lighting equipment controls the amounts of light allowed the birds and facilitates photography. Dr. Cade was relying on his fellow falconers and hawk keepers across the country to make their rare peregrines and other birds available for the breeding experiments.

From the beginning the Cornell ornithologists were determined to do more than simply put a pair of birds into a cage and wait. They also intended to use artificial insemination, which had long been in use in the commercial poultry industry.

On the day I visited the laboratory, there was big news out in the hawk barn. Of seven fertile eggs that had been produced by an artificially inseminated golden eagle, three were hatching. I later learned that one of these young eagles survived. "Within five years," one graduate student told me confidently, "there will be no reason why any bird of prey will have to become extinct." Such programs are only for the most skilled and knowledgeable. Producing such birds is only half the problem; the birds must then be successfully hacked back to the wilds in the hope that they will reinforce the faltering populations in their natural ecosystems—providing those ecosystems are cleared of whatever environmental threats decimated the birds in the first place. It is in this step that some biologists fear the idea will fail and that populations of birds of prey kept too long in captivity may lose their genetic capabilities for survival in the wild.

Across the country, frustrated friends of the eagle lend it aid when granted the opportunity. Congressmen, spurred on by constituents, are quick to express their concern and to point out that they have appropriated funds to aid the rare and endangered species. Federal government biologists at the Patuxent Wildlife Research Center and elsewhere are seeking ways to rescue the eagles. Conservation organizations work to arouse the public conscience and bring to the eagles the same level of concern which has delayed the extinction of the whooping cranes.

But the greatest challenge of all is the need to cleanse the environment of its chemical perils to living species. While there are eagles alive, hope lives also, and where there is hope, and growing concern, there will be no end to the efforts to rescue the endangered eagle from its threatened peril.

15

What of the Future?

On a day in mid-July I sat in the shade of a tree behind Laurel Van Camp's home and talked with him about what had happened to the eagles. Laurel, a long-time employee of Ohio's Division of Wildlife, is a noted authority on the birds of northern Ohio, particularly the birds of prey. His special interest has been the erection of screech owl nest boxes and the banding of more than three thousand young screech owls. But his banding has extended to other species, including the bald eagle.

"Maybe the trouble," he speculated, "is a combination of things. I even wonder if the kinds of trees the eagles have to use for nest trees along Lake Erie today can make any difference. They used to have hickories, oaks, and sycamores. Today many of these trees have been replaced by the weaker, shorter-lived cottonwoods growing on the barrier beaches."

Within half a dozen years he had watched the eagles

along the lake drop from a population of thirteen adult pairs to six. As recently as 1965 he knew of a total of five young raised successfully in the twelve active nests. But the trend was undeniable and perhaps what was happening to the bald eagle was one more symptom of the sickness that had settled over the broad lake from which the eagles had always drawn their food.

In spite of the number of species that have vanished from it, and the massive loads of pollutants sliding down into its basin from contributing waterways, Lake Erie is not, as some people say, "dead." Lake Erie teems with life, but its creatures are no longer a source of clean energy for the threatened eagle.

Each spring, federal and state wildlife workers travel the lakefront by automobile and airplane, searching for the few remaining eagles in order to study their nests. They watch intently for evidence that the old birds are sitting on their skyhigh platforms; when birds are seen at the nests, the eagle watchers return later in the summer and check each eyrie for young. In 1971, when there were only six breeding pairs of eagles left along the lake, Ohio's bald eagle production was one young bird. The following spring the same six pairs of adults were still in residence, occasionally adding sticks to their old nests, then engaging in courtship displays far up in the skies over Lake Erie, and finally producing eggs and incubating them.

But there the story appears to end. In the summer of 1972, for the first time in history, no bald eagle chicks were raised along the Ohio shore.[1] The majestic national bird, symbol of its country's might, was feared to be gone as a breeding species from one more historic area. "I don't see," Laurel Van Camp added, sadly, "how we can possibly have any bald eagles here in another ten years."

Less than 200 years removed from that wilderness world which molded it into the dominant creature it had become, the bald eagle no longer plays its historic role in the Lake Erie ecosystem. Time never freed the eagles completely from their wilderness heritage. They struggled valiantly over the decades and adapted to the changes within the limits of their capacity. But always they gave ground to men.

Those once wild lands lying between Lake Erie and the Ohio River are marked with spreading cities that creep like a malignancy toward each other in all directions. The President's Commission on Population Growth has said that by the year 2000, if the present rate of growth continues, two-thirds of Ohio will be urban in nature, all part of a sprawling megapolis reaching from central New York State on the east to beyond Chicago on the west, a seemingly endless city, population per square mile 300 to 450 people. And throughout that region the eagle will be a memory, an image on a coin, a figure on a weathervane, a piece of plastic, a shadowy figure out of history.[2]

This relationship of eagles to wilderness and the inability of many of them to adapt to the presence of people has been noted by those who have worked closely with the national bird. Nesting failures are most likely near urban and resort areas, lumber camps, and road-building operations.

As people move into an area, the eagles in residence may stay and complete their annual cycle, or even live out their own life span or that of the tree that holds their nest, but they are not likely to rebuild, and new eagles are not likely to replace them as the territory becomes surrounded with human activity. In the long run, people and eagles are not compatible, and the eagles give ground as people move around them.

Increasingly, people have begun invading the most remote nesting territories of the bald eagle in the critical early stages of the nesting effort. "One thing that has been working for the bald eagle in the North Country," Sergej Postupalsky told me, "was the fact that most tourists did not invade the North en masse until about mid-June, after school lets out. By that time breeding eagles were well beyond the critical stage." But this pattern too has been undergoing drastic changes. In the earliest stages of their nesting, when they are incubating eggs or brooding young, there is still snow in the North Woods. With modern snowmobiles, people find the eagle nests—or invade the territory with platoons of roaring, snorting snowmobiles, one more new hazard for the national bird.

Extinction does not come in an instant. It comes in pockets, beginning perhaps with a single territory, where conditions change over weeks or years from optimum, to bearable, to intolerable. These scattered areas increase as pressures grow until they fuse together into larger areas and eventually the species is gone from great segments of its former range—and finally from all of it. It is believed that in 1782, when the bald eagle was designated as the national symbol, it nested in the present location of each of the forty-nine mainland states. But there are no longer mated pairs living in Alabama, Arizona, Arkansas,

Colorado, Connecticut, Delaware, Georgia, Indiana, Iowa, Kansas, Kentucky, Massachusetts, Mississippi, Nebraska, Nevada, New Hampshire, New Jersey, New Mexico, New York, North Dakota, Oklahoma, Rhode Island, South Dakota, Utah, Vermont, or West Virginia. Nor is this the whole story. Several other states have fewer than half a dozen pairs, and most of those, as in Ohio, enjoy scant if any success in producing young.[3]

As the total numbers decline, the death of an individual eagle assumes an increasing seriousness in relation to the remaining population. Today's eagles survive in a chamber of horrors. The hunting parent lifts a sick fish from the water and with it carries along to the nest a new portion of chemical insecticides. And fish may be attached to a tangle of tough monofilament fishing line, in which the young become entangled and die. Another eagle, a young inexperienced bird, meanwhile, falls victim to an automobile. Others drop before thoughtless gunners, are caught in traps, or are methodically executed by sheepmen using poisons, shotguns, traps, and airplanes.

No one knows for certain how many eagles die annually of electrocution. Utility poles make attractive perches for birds of prey, and they are generally safe enough unless their wings span the distance between two power lines. In northern Colorado, Dr. Richard R. Olendorff surveyed the losses of birds of prey beneath high power lines crossing the Pawnee National Grassland and found that electricity had killed at least five birds, mostly golden eagles, along each mile of lines. The only clue to the cause of death are burn marks on the bottom of the feet. In recent years power companies, plagued by blackouts created by wildlife, have been working to make their lines safer for eagles by placing wires farther apart or arranging them in different patterns.[4]

An undetermined number of eagles are still killed each year to obtain their feathers for wearing in ceremonial Indian dances, sometimes by Indians, sometimes by non-Indians.[5] This is usually illegal possession of parts of the eagle, either bald or golden, and can bring a citizen severe fines and jail sentences, but the stealing and dealing continues as eagles are removed from their nests and their skies to supply the feather merchants' demands. An eagle primary feather may bring $5.00, and a talon $2.50. Clandestine dealers appear at the Indian powwows, quietly offering their turkey feathers, and sometimes, to purchasers they can identify, genuine eagle feathers as well. There is even one Indian hobbyist, by no stretch of imagination or geography an Indian, who informed me by mail that he is in a position to supply genuine eagle feathers to his customers in the United States from his place of business in Frankfort, Germany.

More insidious than these recognizable hazards are the invisible pressures exerted on the remaining eagles: stresses from crowding, noise, and environmental pollution, some of them only speculative, inconclusive, and not measurable. There are other factors that can only be revealed by sophisticated chemical analysis of the tissues, among them DDT, DDE, PCBs, and heavy metals. Whether one such agent alone brings death to the individual eagle or they combine in some unfathomed mixture scarcely matters. Total pressures upon the eagles are overwhelming.

There are few places in the United States where the eagle is not immediately threatened. Alaska's eagles seem relatively secure at the moment; the unhatched eggs of Alaska eagles have been found to contain only two parts per million DDT. And in the southern tip of Florida, mainly within the boundaries of the Everglades National Park, lives perhaps the only secure, healthy population of southern bald eagles anywhere. But between these two distant corners of the United States, the future of the bald eagle is filled with peril. Even in Florida, beyond the boundaries of the Everglades, the eagles seem to be slowly losing ground, and there is little long-range hope for them along either coast to the north. In Texas, Dr. Clarence Cottam, director of the Welder Wildlife Foundation and former assistant chief of the Bureau of Sport Fisheries and Wildlife, observes that "following World War II, bald eagles nested rather commonly in eastern Texas, but that few nests are left today, and fewer still that produce any young."[6] Throughout the United States this account is repeated, and biologists who have watched the demise of the bald eagle come back repeatedly to three basic causes: "hard" pesticides, shooting, and the disappearance of suitable breeding areas.

The "hard" pesticides, the chlorinated hydrocarbons, should be outlawed.[7] The shooting must be halted, with educational campaigns and increased law enforcement, after the manner of the long and successful effort in behalf of the whooping crane. The nesting areas must be protected and unused nests must be preserved, in the hope that immature birds might return and establish eyries.

If these aims can be accomplished, and if the contamination of the environment can be curbed, remnants of the eagles that were our heritage may be among us for years to come. But as of this writing their numbers still fall, and rescue efforts are inadequate. Even if we could cease the use at once of the chemical biocides, years must pass before the ecosystem could be clean again.[8] There may be, as John Mathisen says, a glimmer of hope: "The solution is at least within the grasp of man."

REFERENCE NOTES

SELECTED BIBLIOGRAPHY

ACKNOWLEDGMENTS

INDEX

Reference Notes

1. THE NATIONAL BIRD

1. Edward H. Forbush, *Birds of Massachusetts and Other New England States* (Massachusetts Department of Agriculture, 1927), Part II, pp. 151–52.
2. *Bald Eagles of the Chippewa National Forest* (Grand Rapids, Minnesota: *Grand Rapids Herald Review*, 1971), pp. 3–5.
3. John Mathisen and Jack Stewart, "A Band for an Eagle," *The Loon*, September, 1970, p. 84.
4. Alexander Sprunt IV, "Audubon Bald Eagle Studies, 1960–1966," *Proceedings of the 62nd Annual Convention of the National Audubon Society*, November 12, 1966.
5. E. Adamson Hoebel, *The Cheyennes: Indians of the Great Plains* (Holt, Rinehart and Winston, 1960), p. 67.
6. Gaillard Hunt, "History of the Seal of the United States," *Journals of Congress*, vol. 517 (1906), p. 7.
7. *Ibid.*
8. Benjamin Franklin, *The Complete Works of Benjamin Franklin*, ed. John Bigelow (New York and London: G. P. Putnam's Sons, 1887–8), X, 279.
9. J. M. Williams, *The Eagle Regiment* (Belleville, Wis.: Recorder Printing, 1890), pp. 1–166.

2. THE VANISHING WILDERNESS

1. Francis H. Herrick, *The American Eagle* (New York and London: D. Appleton-Century Company, 1934), pp. 15–16.
2. E. Lucy Braun, *Deciduous Forests of Eastern North America* (New York: Hafner Publishing Company, 1967), p. 35.
3. *Magee Marsh Wildlife Area: Cradle of Wildlife* (Columbus, Ohio: Ohio Department of Natural Resources, [n.d.]), p. 4.
4. *The Ohio Guide* (New York: Oxford University Press, 1940), p. 219.
5. *Ibid.*
6. R. Carlyle Buley, *The Old Northwest Pioneer Period 1815–1840* (Indianapolis: Indiana Historical Society, 1950), I, 162.
7. *The Ohio Guide*, p. 374.

8. *Ibid.*, p. 219

9. Betty Trinter, *The Way It Was* (Norwalk, Ohio: Eberts, Inc., 1965), p. 26.

3. THE EAGLE FAMILY

1. Leslie Brown and Dean Amadon, *Eagles, Hawks, and Falcons of the World.* 2 vols. (New York: McGraw-Hill Book Company, 1968), I, 279–99.

2. "Vanishing Sea Eagles Raise Only One Young," *Conservation around the Globe,* World Wildlife Fund, Press Release No. 1372, p. 2.

3. John G. Williams, *A Field Guide to the Birds of East and Central Africa* (London: William Collins Sons and Co., 1963), pp. 59–60.

4. Chandler S. Robbins, Bertel Bruun, and Herbert S. Zim, *Birds of North America: A Guide to Field Identification* (New York: Golden Press, 1966), p. 76.

5. Pierce Brodkorb, "Number of Feathers and Weights of Various Systems in a Bald Eagle," *Wilson Bulletin,* LXVII, No. 2 (June, 1955), 142.

6. Howard E. Eaton, *Birds of New York,* Part II (Albany: The University of the State of New York, 1914), p. 92.

7. G. L. Walls, *The Vertebrate Eye and Its Adaptive Radiation* (Bloomfield Hills, Mich.: The Cranbrook Press, 1942), pp. 641–62.

8. Elton Fawks, "A Survey of Wintering Bald Eagles," *Iowa Bird Life,* XXX, No. 3 (September, 1960), 56–58.

9. William E. Southern, "Additional Observations on Winter Bald Eagle Populations: Including Remarks on Biotelemetry Techniques and Immature Plumages," *The Wilson Bulletin,* LXXVI, No. 2 (June, 1964), 134.

10. Joel Carl Welty, *The Life of Birds* (Philadelphia and London: W. B. Saunders Company, 1962), pp. 170–71.

11. Milton B. Trautman, *Birds of Buckeye Lake, Ohio,* Museum of Zoology, University of Michigan, Miscellaneous Publication No. 44, 1940, pp. 217–18.

12. Brown and Amadon, I, pp. 99–100.

4. THE EYRIE

1. Francis H. Herrick, *The American Eagle* (New York: D. Appleton-Century Company, 1934), pp. 1–2.

2. Richard J. Hensel and Willard A. Troyer, "Nesting Studies of the Bald Eagle in Alaska," *The Condor*, LXVI, No. 4 (July–August, 1964), 282.

3. Olaus J. Murie, *Fauna of the Aleutian Islands and Alaska Peninsula*, U.S. Fish and Wildlife Service, North American Fauna Series, No. 61, 1959, p. 114.

4. Myrtle Jeanne Broley, *Eagle Man* (New York: Pellegrini and Cudahy, 1952), p. 66.

5. Charles L. Broley, "Migration and Nesting of Florida Bald Eagles," *The Wilson Bulletin*, LIX, No. 1 (March, 1947), 17–18.

6. William R. Meiners, *Snake River Birds of Prey Natural Area: A Pictorial Resume Indicative of the Needs for Protective Withdrawal*, (U.S. Bureau of Land Management, 1970), p. 26.

7. Jackson Miles Abbott, "Status Report on the Bald Eagle," *Virginia Wildlife*, July, 1962, pp. 4–6.

8. Herrick, pp. 116–17.

9. Arthur C. Bent, *Life Histories of North American Birds of Prey*, Smithsonian Institution, Bulletin 167, 1937, Part I, p. 115.

10. Charles L. Broley, "Migration and Nesting of Florida Bald Eagles," p. 10.

5. THE EAGLES OF VERMILION

1. Francis H. Herrick, *The American Eagle* (New York: D. Appleton-Century Company, 1934), pp. 2–3.

2. *Ibid.*, p. 8.

3. *Ibid.*, p. 38.

6. A MATTER OF DIET

1. Francis H. Herrick, *The American Eagle* (New York: D. Appleton–Century Company, 1934), pp. 10–12.

2. Arthur C. Bent, *Life Histories of North American Birds of Prey*, Smithsonian Institution, Bulletin 167, 1937, Part I, p. 330.

3. Richard R. Olendorff, "Sheep, Eagles, and Power Lines," *Colorado Outdoors*, January–February, 1972, pp. 5–6.

4. Herrick, p. 72.

5. Bent, p. 328.

6. Karl W. Kenyon, "Isolation Protects the Bald Eagle in Alaska," *Audubon*, September–October, 1961, pp. 273–74.

7. Bent, p. 330.
8. *Ibid.*, p. 328.
9. *Ibid.*, p. 329.
10. Herrick, pp. 164–65.

7. THE CHAMPION EAGLE BANDER

1. Myrtle Jeanne Broley, *Eagle Man* (New York: Pellegrini and Cudahy, 1952), pp. 3–12.
2. Roger T. Peterson, *Birds over America* (New York: Dodd, Mead, & Company, 1964), pp. 122–34.
3. Myrtle Jeanne Broley, pp. 31–34.
4. Charles L. Broley, "Migration and Nesting of the Florida Bald Eagles," *The Wilson Bulletin*, LIX, No. 1 (March, 1947), 20.
5. Myrtle Jeanne Broley, pp. 153–55.
6. Charles L. Broley, "The Plight of the Florida Bald Eagle," *Audubon*, January–February, 1950, p. 48.
7. Myrtle Jeanne Broley, p. xiii.
8. Charles L. Broley, "The Plight of the American Bald Eagle," *Audubon*, July–August, 1958, p. 162.
9. *Ibid.*
10. Richard L. Cunningham, "The Status of the Bald Eagle in Florida," *Audubon*, January–February, 1960, p. 25.

8. DANGER IN THE SKY

1. Walter R. Spofford, *The Golden Eagle in the Trans-Pecos and Edwards Plateau of Texas*, National Audubon Society, Conservation Report No. 1, 1964, pp. 11–12.
2. W. W. Johnson, "Texas Eagle Chowser," *Life*, June 13, 1949, pp. 2–13.
3. Frederick H. Dale, "Eagle 'Control' in Northern California," *The Condor*, XXXVIII (September, 1936), 208.
4. *Ibid.*, 209.
5. Spofford, p. 31.
6. *Ibid.*, p. 30.
7. *Ibid.*, p. 17.

9. THE CHEMICAL AGE

1. F. C. Bishopp, "The Tax We Pay to Insects," *Science in Farming*, U.S. Department of Agriculture Yearbook, 1943–47, p. 614.
2. H. L. Haller and Ruth L. Busbey, "The Chemistry of DDT," *Science in Farming*, U.S. Department of Agriculture Yearbook, 1943–47, p. 616.
3. *Ibid.*
4. Neil Hotchkiss and Richard H. Pough, "Effects on Forest Birds of DDT Used for Gypsy Moth Control in Pennsylvania," *The Journal of Wildlife Management*, X, No. 3 (July, 1946), p. 202–7.
5. Bishopp, p. 615.
6. Gaylord Nelson, *Congressional Record*, 92nd Congress, First Session, CXVII, No. 51 (April 14, 1971), p. 10399.
7. *Ibid.*
8. Joseph A. Hagar, "History of the Massachusetts Peregrine Falcon Population, 1935–57," in J. J. Hickey (ed.), *Peregrine Falcon Populations* (Madison, Wis.: The University of Wisconsin Press, 1969), pp. 128–30.
9. Rachel Carson, *Silent Spring* (Boston: Houghton Mifflin Company, 1962), p. 262–75.
10. Lonnie L. Williamson (ed.), "Pesticides Fail in Mosquito Control," *Outdoor News Bulletin*, Wildlife Management Institute, January 7, 1972, p. 2.
11. *Pesticide Wildlife Studies: A Review of Fish and Wildlife Service Investigations during 1961–62*, U.S. Bureau of Sport Fisheries and Wildlife, p. 79.
12. George Laycock, "Beginning of the End for DDT," *Audubon*, July, 1969, p. 38.
13. D. A. Ratcliffe, "Decrease in Eggshell Weights in Certain Birds of Prey," *Nature*, CCXV (July 8, 1967), 210.
14. *Fish, Wildlife and Pesticides*, U.S. Bureau of Sport Fisheries and Wildlife (Washington, D.C.: U.S. Government Printing Office, [n.d.]), p. 9.
15. Laycock, p. 39.
16. *Ibid.*, p. 38.
17. Ray Coppock, "Dramatic New Evidence of Pesticide Damage," *U.C. News*, University of California, Berkeley, May 25, 1971, p. 1.
18. Stanley N. Wiemeyer and Richard D. Porter, "DDE Thins Egg Shells of Captive American Kestrels," *Nature*, CCXXVII, No. 5259 (August 15, 1970), 737–38.
19. *Fish, Wildlife and Pesticides*, p. 7.

20. Joseph J. Hickey (ed.), *Peregrine Falcon Populations: Their Biology and Decline* (Madison, Wis.: The University of Wisconsin Press, 1969), p. 465.

21. *Environmental Quality: The First Annual Report of the Council on Environmental Quality* (Washington, D.C.: U.S. Government Printing Office, 1970), p. 131.

22. Frank Graham, Jr., *Since Silent Spring* (Boston: Houghton Mifflin Company, 1970), pp. 141–43.

23. L. F. Stickel *et. al.*, "Bald Eagle Pesticide Relations" (abstract), 31st North American Wildlife and Natural Resources Conference, Wildlife Management Institute, 1966.

24. "Eagles in Maine Being Wiped Out by Environmental Pollutants According to Audubon Society Study," National Audubon Society News Release, August 10, 1970, p. 1.

25. *Ibid.*, pp. 1–2.

26. Sergej Postupalsky, *Toxic Chemicals and Declining Bald Eagles and Cormorants in Ontario* (Madison, Wis.: Department of Wildlife Ecology, University of Wisconsin, 1971), p. 12.

27. Kevin P. Shea, "Old Weapons Are Best," *Environment*, XIII, No. 5 (June, 1971), 49.

28. Clarence Cottam, personal correspondence, November 2, 1972.

10. A SEARCH FOR EAGLES

1. Elton Fawks, "A Survey of the Wintering Bald Eagles 1960–61," *Iowa Bird Life*, XXXI, No. 3 (September, 1961), p. 55.

2. Joseph J. Hickey (ed.), *Peregrine Falcon Populations: Their Biology and Decline* (Madison, Wis.: The University of Wisconsin Press, 1969), p. 349.

3. Laurence Isard, "Ohio's Bald Eagles: Can They Survive?" *The Explorer* (Cleveland Natural Science Museum), IX, No. 3, p. 4.

4. L. Krumlien and N. Hollister, *The Birds of Wisconsin* (Madison, Wis.: Wisconsin Society for Ornithology, 1951), p. 122.

5. Ira N. Gabrielson and Stanley G. Jewett, *Birds of the Pacific Northwest* (New York: Dover Publications, Inc., 1970), p. 196.

6. Alexander Sprunt IV and Frank J. Ligas, "Audubon Bald Eagle Studies," reprinted from *Proceedings of the 62nd Annual Convention of the National Audubon Society*, 1966, p. 25.

7. *Ibid.*, p. 1.

8. Elton Fawks, "A Survey of Wintering Bald Eagles," *Iowa Bird Life*, XXX, No. 3 (September, 1960), 56.
9. Sprunt and Ligas, p. 2.
10. Alexander Sprunt IV and Frank J. Ligas, Continental Bald Eagle Project Progress Report No. 3, National Audubon Society, 1963, reprinted from *Proceedings of the 59th Annual Convention of the National Audubon Society*, 1963, pp. 2–7.
11. William B. Robertson, personal correspondence.
12. Alexander Sprunt IV, "Bald Eagles Aren't Producing Enough Young," *Audubon*, January–February 1963, p. 33.

11. INTOLERANCE AND POISON

1. United States Senate Hearings, *Predator Control and Related Problems*, Subcommittee on Agriculture, Environmental, and Consumer Protection of the Committee on Appropriations, 92nd Congress, First Session, June 2, 1971, testimony of Nathaniel P. Reed, p. 25.
2. Charles H. Callison, "A Massacre of Eagles," *Audubon*, July, 1971, p. 94.
3. Senate Hearings, *Predator Control . . .* , First Session, June 2–3, 1971, pp. 1–143.
4. *Ibid.*, pp. 23–34.
5. "Eagle Briefs," *High Country News*, August 8, 1971, p. 11.
6. Senate Hearings, *Predator Control . . .* , First Session, June 2–3, 1971, testimony of Charles H. Lawrence, pp. 41–44.
7. Charles H. Callison, "Eagles Are Protected by Federal Law," *Audubon*, September, 1971, p. 109.
8. Tom Bell, *High Country News*, May 28, 1971, p. 2.
9. National Audubon Society News Release, September 7, 1971, p. 2.
10. Senate Hearings, *Predator Control . . .* , Second Session, December 17, 1971, testimony of Sander Orent, pp. 332–92.
11. *Predator Control—1971*, Report to the [President's] Council on Environmental Quality, January, 1972, pp. 5–14.
12. Senate Hearings, *Predator Control . . .* , First Session, June 2, 1971, p. 100.
13. *Ibid.*, p. 102.
14. *Casper* (Wyoming) *Star-Tribune*, May 18, 1972, p. 1.

12. SHOTGUNS AND HELICOPTERS

1. United States Senate Hearings, *Predator Control and Related Problems,* Subcommittee on Agriculture, Environmental, and Consumer Protection of the Committee on Appropriations, 92nd Congress, First Session, August 2, 1971, testimony of Senator Gale McGee, p. 173.
2. *Ibid.,* testimony of James O. Vogan, p. 192.
3. *Ibid.,* p. 164.
4. *Ibid.,* p. 191.
5. *Ibid.,* testimony of Nathaniel P. Reed, p. 170.
6. *Conservation News,* National Wildlife Federation, XXXVIII, No. 1 (January 1, 1973), 3–4.
7. Fred C. Robards and James G. King, *Nesting and Productivity of Bald Eagles: Southeast Alaska,* U.S. Bureau of Sport Fisheries and Wildlife, 1966, p. 3.
8. *Predator Control—1971,* Report to the [President's] Council on Environmental Quality, January, 1972, p. 9.
9. Senate Hearings, Predator Control . . . , First Session, June 3, 1971, testimony of Russell E. Train, p. 112.

13. LAND OF MANY EAGLES

1. George Laycock, *Alaska: The Embattled Frontier* (Boston: Houghton Mifflin Company, 1971), p. 41.
2. Charles Sprague Sargent, *Manual of the Trees of North America,* I, 41–2.
3. Fred C. Robards and James G. King, *Nesting and Productivity of Bald Eagles: Southeast Alaska,* U.S. Bureau of Sport Fisheries and Wildlife, 1966, p. 2.
4. *Ibid.,* pp. 4–5.
5. *Ibid.,* pp. 9–10.
6. Laycock, *Alaska,* p. 53.

14. FIRST AID AND DEEP CONCERN

1. "America, The Upside Down Eagle," *The Florida Naturalist,* XLV, No. 1 (February, 1972), 22–24.

2. "Bald Eagle Survives Shooting, Information Rewarded," *Conservation News*, National Wildlife Federation, June 1, 1972, p. 10.

3. Thad L. Fuller, personal correspondence.

4. *Weyerhaeuser World*, January, 1972, p. 8–9.

5. Dorothy Beckworth, "What About Those Florida Audubon Sanctuaries?" *The Florida Naturalist*, XLIII, No. 2 (April, 1970), 58–59.

6. Francis H. Herrick, *The American Eagle* (New York: D. Appleton-Century Company, 1934), pp. 113–15.

7. Nancy Hicks, "Upstate Biology Professor, 'Thinking Like a Bird,' Breeds the Rare Peregrine Falcon in Captivity," *New York Times*, June 10, 1971, p. C31.

15. WHAT OF THE FUTURE?

1. Richard C. Branzell, "Bald Eagle Production Survey: Ohio," U.S. Bureau of Sport Fisheries and Wildlife, May 5, 1972.

2. *Population and the American Future: A Report of the Commission on Population Growth and the American Future*, (Washington, D.C.: U.S. Government Printing Office, March 16, 1972), p. 33.

3. Alexander Sprunt IV, personal interview.

4. Richard R. Olendorff, "Sheep, Eagles, and Power Lines," *Colorado Outdoors*, January–February 1972, pp. 5–6.

5. Ben East, "State's Eagles Face a New Threat," *The Sunday News* (Detroit), July 25, 1971, p. 6-D.

6. Clarence Cottam, personal correspondence, November 2, 1972.

7. George Laycock, "Beginning of the End for DDT," *Audubon*, July, 1969, p. 43.

8. *Environmental Quality*, The Council on Environmental Quality, First Annual Report, August, 1970, p. 132.

Selected Bibliography

Bent, Arthur C. *Life Histories of North American Birds of Prey*, Vol. I. New York: Dover Publications, Inc., 1961. (Originally published as Smithsonian Institution Bulletin 167, 1937).

Braun, E. Lucy. *Deciduous Forests of Eastern North America*. New York: Hafner Publishing Co., 1967.

Broley, Charles L. "The Plight of the American Bald Eagle," *Audubon*, July, 1958, pp. 162–63.

———. "The Plight of the Florida Bald Eagle," *Audubon*, January, 1950, pp. 42–49.

———. "Migration and Nesting of Florida Bald Eagles," *Wilson Bulletin*, LIX, No. 1 (1947), 3–20.

Broley, Myrtle Jeanne. *Eagle Man*. New York: Pellegrini and Cudahy, 1952.

Brown, Leslie. *Eagles*. New York: Arco Publishing Co., 1970.

Brown, Leslie, and Amadon, Dean. *Eagles, Hawks, and Falcons of the World*. 2 vols. New York: McGraw-Hill Book Company, 1968.

Carson, Rachel. *Silent Spring*. Boston: Houghton Mifflin Company, 1962.

Gordon, Robert B. *Natural Vegetation of Ohio in Pioneer Days*. Ohio Biological Survey Series, Vol. III, No. 2. Columbus: Ohio State University Press, 1969.

Graham, Frank, Jr. *Since Silent Spring*. Boston: Houghton Mifflin Company, 1970.

Herrick, Francis H. *The American Eagle: A Study in Natural and Civil History*. New York: D. Appleton-Century Company, 1934.

———. "An Eagle Observatory," *Auk*, XLI (1924), 89–105.

———. "Nests and Nesting of the American Eagle," *Auk*, XLI (1924), 213–31.

———. "The Daily Life of the American Eagle: Late Phase," *Auk*, XLI (1924), 389–422.

———. "The Daily Life of the American Eagle: Late Phase Concluded," *Auk*, XLI (1924), 517–41.

Hickey, Joseph J. (ed.). *Peregrine Falcon Populations: Their Biology and Decline*. Madison, Wis.: University of Wisconsin Press, 1969.

Howe, Henry. *Historical Collections of Ohio in Two Volumes, An Encyclopedia of the State*. . . . Cincinnati: C. J. Krehbiel & Co., 1907.

Hunt, Gaillard. *The History of the Seal of the United States*. Washington: U.S. Department of State, 1909.

Laycock, George. *Alaska: The Embattled Frontier*. Boston: Houghton Mifflin Company, 1971.

Peterson, Roger T. *Birds over North America*. New York: Dodd, Mead & Company, 1948.

Spofford, Walter R. *The Golden Eagle in the Trans-Pecos and Edwards Plateau of Texas.* Audubon Conservation Report No. 1. New York: National Audubon Society, 1964.

Sprunt, Alexander, IV. *Continental Bald Eagle Progress Reports,* Nos. 1, 2, 3. New York: National Audubon Society, 1961, 1962, 1963.

Welty, Joel C. *The Life of Birds.* Philadelphia: W. B. Saunders Company, 1962.

Acknowledgments

THE AUTHOR is especially grateful to those generous individuals who granted time for interviews, invited him to accompany them on field trips, provided research data, or read the completed manuscript. Among those deserving special mention are Alexander Sprunt IV, National Audubon Society; C. Eugene Knoder, National Audubon Society; Sergej Postupalsky, Department of Wildlife Ecology, University of Wisconsin; Dr. William B. Robertson, Jr., Everglades National Park; Fred Robards, U.S. Game Management Agent, Juneau, Alaska; John Mathisen, Wildlife Biologist, U.S. Forest Service; Everett L. Sutton, U.S. Bureau of Sport Fisheries and Wildlife; Dr. Walter R. Spofford, Etna, New York; Dr. Clarence Cottam, Welder Wildlife Foundation; John M. Anderson, National Audubon Society; Laurel Van Camp, Ohio Division of Wildlife; Dr. Milton B. Trautman, Ohio State University Museum of Zoology; Dr. Ray C. Erickson, Patuxent Wildlife Research Center; Karl H. Maslowski; Richard H. Pough; Jackson M. Abbott; Elton Fawks; John B. Holt; Jack Stewart.

Grateful acknowledgment for permission to use photographs is made to: G. Ronald Austing (pages 8, 30); Erwin A. Bauer (page 14); Case Western Reserve University (pages 10, 11, 12); Karl H. Maslowski (pages 13, 16, 17, 18, 19, 20, 21, 22, 29); Michigan Department of Commerce (page 28). Thanks for assistance in gathering photographs are also due to Ruth W. Helmuth, archivist, Case Western Reserve University, and to Clarence W. Koch. Photographs not otherwise acknowledged were taken by the author.

Index

Abbott, Jackson M., 148

Adams, John, 47

Advisory Committee on Predator Control, 189

Agassiz National Refuge, 204

Aldrin, 146

American Ornithological Union, 108

American Smelting and Refining Company, 165

Anderson, John M., 94–95

Army Corps of Engineers, 207

Atomic Energy Commission, 198

Audubon, (magazine), 150, 162

Audubon Society:
  Florida, 201–202, 203, 206–207
  Murie (Caspar, Wyo.), 161, 177, 179
  National, 43, 94, 108, 109, 127, 144, 149–151, 161–162, 168, 171, 175, 177

Baker, John W., 103, 149, 150

bald eagle, *see* eagle, bald

Bald Eagle Act, 126, 130

Barton, William, 47–48

Beecham, John, 172–173

Bell, Tom, 169

Bent, Arthur C., 105

Bering, Vitus, 60

Big Bend Eagle Club, 123–124

Big Bend National Park, 128

Bird banding, 41–42, 107–121, 155, 212

Bishopp, F. C., 132, 134

Boise Cascade, 207

bounty system in Alaska, 187–188, 194

Braun, E. Lucy, 53

Brewster, William, 105

Brodkorb, Pierce, 65

Broley, Charles L., 77, 79, 80, 107–108, 110–121, 132, 135, 148, 150, 157, 158

Broley, Myrtle, 108, 150

Brooks Range, 38

Broun, Maurice, 147–148

Buckheister, Carl, 127

Buffalo Zoological Gardens, 209

Bureau of Land Management, 156, 207

Bureau of Sport Fisheries and Wildlife, 40, 104, 146, 150, 156, 163, 166–167, 176, 194, 195, 197, 204, 207, 218
  Division of Management and Enforcement, 162, 186
  Division of Wildlife Services, 170, 174, 175, 176

Buss, Gary, 204

Cade, Tom J., 209–210

Cain Committee, 189–190

Callison, Charles H., 162, 178

Carson, Rachel, 120, 137

Carter, Lorenzo, 56

Case Western Reserve University, 89, 92

Casparis, John, 122–125

Centennial Valley, 38

Chippewa National Forest, 39, 43, 44, 154

Cincinnatus, Order of, 48

Cleaveland, General Moses, 55–56

Cleveland Academy of Natural Sciences, 148

Cleveland Museum of Natural History, 95–96

Colorado Cooperative Wildlife Research Unit, 172
Colorado State University, 100, 172
Compound 1080, 163, 165, 176
Connecticut Land Co., 55
Continental Bald Eagle Project, 150, 154, 158–159
Cooperative Bald Eagle Sanctuary, 206
Copeland, A. D., 95–96
Cornell University, 127, 141, 209
Cottam, Clarence, 146, 218
Craighead, John, 172
Crandall, F. A., 209
Culex tarsalis, 136
Cunningham, Richard L., 149
cyanide, 164, 165

Dale, Frederick H., 125, 126
DDE, 141, 142, 143, 144, 217
DDT, 120, 132–146, 199, 217, 218
Department of Agriculture, 132, 133, 137, 145, 170
dieldrin, 140, 144, 146
Dunstan, Thomas 39

eagle:
    African fish, 61
    bald: animals sharing the nest of, 79–80; behavior at nest, 38–39, 41–42, 64–65, 71, 82, 83, 106, 112–113; breeding in captivity, 208–209; chick, description, 64; compatibility with people, 214–215; courtship display, 73–74; decline of, 43–44, 57–58, 109, 118–121, 132, 138, 144–146, 148–149, 152–153, 177, 199, 212–219; description of, 38, 39, 63–68, 84; diet of, 97–105, 131, 169–173,

198–199; division into subspecies, 63–64; fighting, 70; hazards to, 118, 206–207, 216–218; incubation, 82–83, 84; juveniles, 64–65, 71, 106, 110, 112–113; longevity, 64; migration, 68–69, 110, 129, 151–153, 160; molt, 65; monogamy, 64; nest, description and location, 76–79, 84–87, 89, 115–116, 155, 196, 200; nesting, 76–87, 117, 200; number of, 152–153, 156–159, 198, 199, 213–214; "Old Abe," 49–51; poisoning of, 130, 162–168; range, 43–44, 152–153; roosting, 69; sheep killing, 169–173; soaring, 72–73; sterility, 120, 138, 144, 149, 158, 213–214; symbol of the U.S., 46–49, 62; Vermilion eagles, 52–55, 57, 58, 84, 88–96; vision, 66–67; voice, 65–66; winter census of, 151–153
    golden, 62–63, 73–74, 81, 100, 125, 126, 127, 130, 162, 171, 172, 182, 185, 216, 217
    harpy, 59
    little, 59
    Madagascar fish, 62
    monkey-eating, 59
    number of species, 59–60
    Pallas sea, 62
    Stanford's sea, 61
    Stellar's, 60
    white-bellied sea, 62
    white-tailed sea, 60–61
Eaton, Howard E., 66
Everglades National Park, 156–157, 218

falconers, 67, 209

Fawks, Elton, 147, 150–151
Forest and Stream, 208
Forest Service, U.S., 41, 150, 156, 195, 197
Forbush, Edward H., 39
Franklin, Benjamin, 47–49
Fraternal Order of Eagles, 154
Frenzel, L.D., Jr., 40

Gabrielson, Ira N., 148
Garrett, R. L., 141
grazing permits, 189–190
Great Lakes Historical Society, 95
Grewe, Alfred, Jr., 39

Hager, Joseph A., 135
Haller, H. L., 133
Hathaway, Stanley K., 163, 176, 180
Hawk Mountain Sanctuary, 147–148
Head, Cliff, 201–202
Hensel, Richard J., 76
heptachlor epoxide, 144, 146
Herrick, Francis H., 83, 88–96, 98–99, 102, 109
Heugly, Leo G., 172
Hickel, Walter J., 180
High Country News, 169
Holt, John B. (Jack), 79, 84, 86, 154–155, 205
Horne, Dale, 180
Hotchkiss, Neil, 133
Hulse, Henry, 208
Hutchinson, Tom, 167

International Union for the Conservation of Nature, 59
Irvine, Van, 168, 181
Izaak Walton League of America, 98

Jefferson, Thomas, 47
Jewett, Stanley G., 149
Johnson, Joe, 194
Johnson, Norm, 167
Journal of Wildlife Management, 133
Juenemann, Greg, 39

Kenyon, Karl, 104
Kerr, Ewing T., 186
King, James, 195–196, 198
Knoder, C. Eugene, 144
Kodiak National Wildlife Refuge, 76
Krause, Gordon, 161, 167
Kussman, Joel, 39

Lawrence, Charles H., 162, 167, 178–179, 181
Ligas, Frank, 144

Maslowski, Karl H., 94
Mathisen, John, 39–44, 154, 219
McCann, Daniel, 50
McCutchen, Richard, 170–171
McFarland, L. Z., 141
McGahan, Jerry, 172
McGee, Gale, 163, 179, 181, 183
McGinnis, James, 50–51
Meiners, William, 81
Meng, Heinz, 209
methyl parathion, 136
mirex, 146
Morgan, Sid O., 194
Murie, Olaus J., 77

National Park Service, 150, 156
National Wildlife Federation, 203
Necedah National Wildlife Refuge, 204
Nelson, Morlan, 81

Nolta, Floyd, 126
Northern States Power Co., 207

official seal, U.S., 47–48
Ohio Division of Wildlife, 212
Ohio Fish and Game Commission, 98
Olendorff, Richard R., 100, 216
oologists, 109
Orent, Sander, 173–174

parathion, 136
Patuxent Wildlife Research Center, 86,
    138, 139, 144, 163, 165, 210
PCBs, 144, 217
Peakall, David, 141
Peterson, Roger T., 109
Postupalsky, Sergej, 79, 86, 144, 154,
    205, 215
Pough, Richard H., 107–110, 114, 117,
    133
Predator Ecology Laboratory, 173
President's Commission on Population
    Growth, 214
President's Council on Environmental
    Quality, 175, 189, 191
primitive man, 44–46

Radcliffe, Derek A., 138–139
Red Data Book, 59
Reed, Nathaniel, 162, 178, 184, 185
Richmond, Doug, 187
Ritter, Willard E., 180
Robards, Fred, 102–103, 192, 194–200
Robertson, William B. Jr., 167–157
Robinson, Cecil, 120
Routt National Forest, 173

Silent Spring, 120, 137
sodium fluoroacetate, 163

Southern, William E., 69
Spofford, Walter R., 127–130, 171–
    172
Sprunt, Alexander, IV, 43, 150–151,
    154, 158–159, 168, 175–176
State College, New Paltz, N.Y., 209
St. Cloud College, 39
Steller, Georg Wilhelm, 60
Stewart, Jack, 40–43, 76
strychnine, 163–164, 165, 174
Sutton, Everett L., 186
Swope Park Zoo, 209

thallium sulfate, 164, 165, 166, 167,
    180
thinness of egg shells, 139, 141–142
Thompson, Charles, 48
Thunder of Bees, Chief, 50
Tongas National Forest, 192–193
Torey, Ben, 125, 126
tower-building, 90–91, 93–94, 204–
    205, 206
toxaphene, 136
Train, Russell E., 191
Trautman, Milton B., 70–76
tree climbing, 40–42, 110–113, 117–
    118, 154–155
Troyer, Willard A., 76
Turner, Robert K., 161–162

University of California, Davis, 141
University of Florida, 65
University of Michigan, 173
University of Strasbourg, 134
University of Wisconsin, 139, 144–145

Van Camp, Laurel, 86, 212–214
Vaughan, Doyle, 181, 183, 186
Vermilion, Ohio, eagles, *see* eagle, bald

Vogan, James O., 181–185, 191

Wampler, Bruce, 161, 167
Welder Wildlife Foundation, 146, 218
Werner, Herman, 181, 184–185
Western Reserve University, *see* Case
    Western Reserve University
Weyerhaeuser Co, 206, 207

Wilson, Alexander, 104
World Wildlife Fund, 154
Wyoming Cooperative Crop and Live-
    stock Reporting Service, 170
Wyoming Game and Fish Commission,
    167
Wyoming Stock Growers Association,
    168

About the Author

George Laycock has traveled extensively throughout North and South America, studying animals in their natural habitats. He is a Field Editor for *Audubon* Magazine, and his articles have also appeared in *Field and Stream, Better Homes and Gardens,* and other national magazines. His numerous books include *Sign of the Flying Goose, The Diligent Destroyers,* and *Alaska: The Embattled Frontier.*